D0997430

F*CK

F*CK

The History of the World in 65 Unfortunate Incidents

Martin Rawson

UNIVERSE

First published in the United States of America in 2009 by
Universe Publishing
A Division of Rizzoli International Publications, Inc.
300 Park Avenue South
New York, NY 10010
www.rizzoliusa.com

Originally published in the United Kingdom in 2008 by
Jonathan Cape, Random House,
20 Vauxhall Bridge Road
London SW1V 2SA

2009 2010 2011 2012 / 10 9 8 7 6 5 4 3 2 1

ISBN: 978-0-7893-2057-5

Library of Congress Control Number: 2009901498

Printed in Singapore

As ever, for Anna, Fred, and Rose

The Big Bang

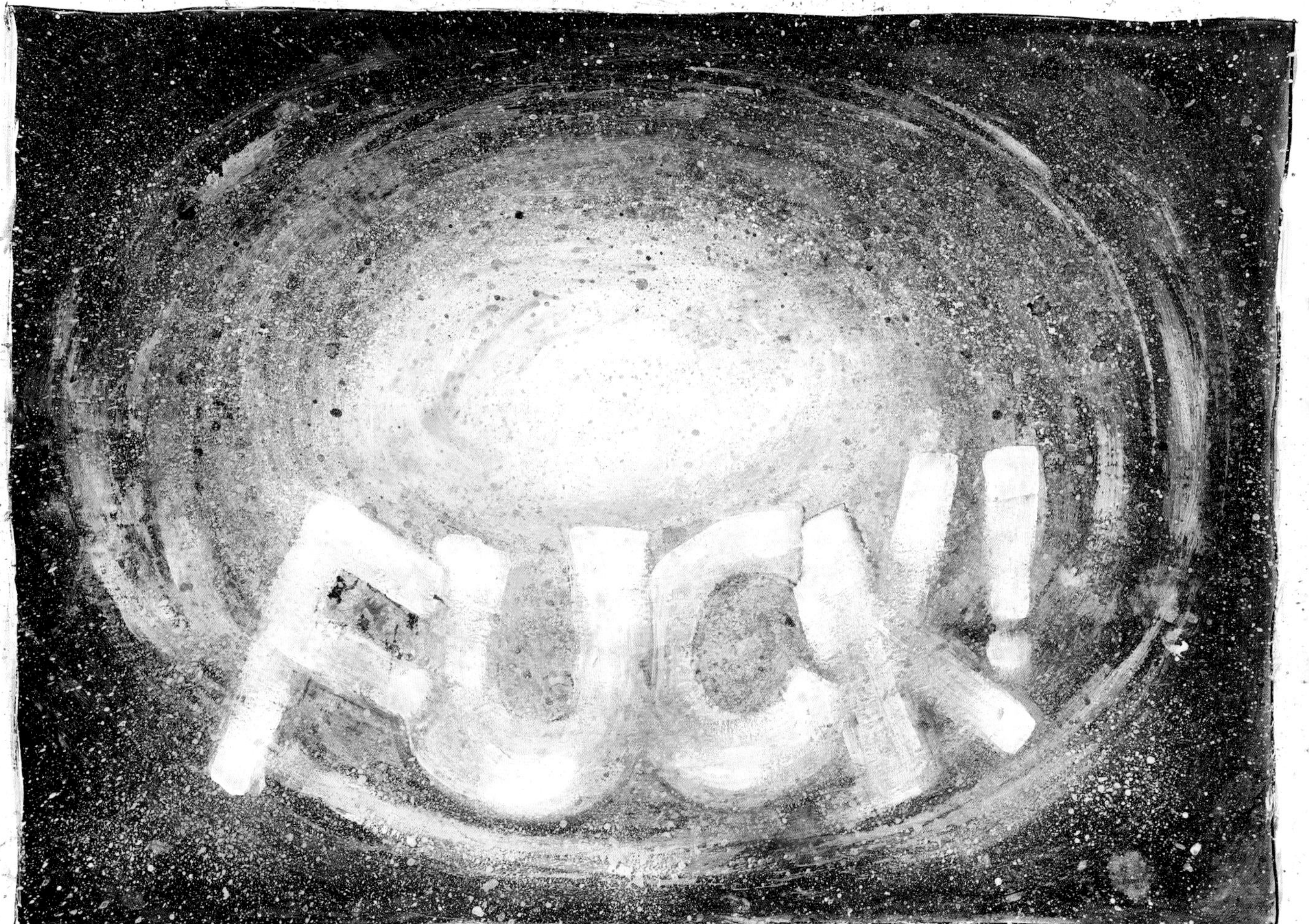
FUCK!

The Formation of the Solar System

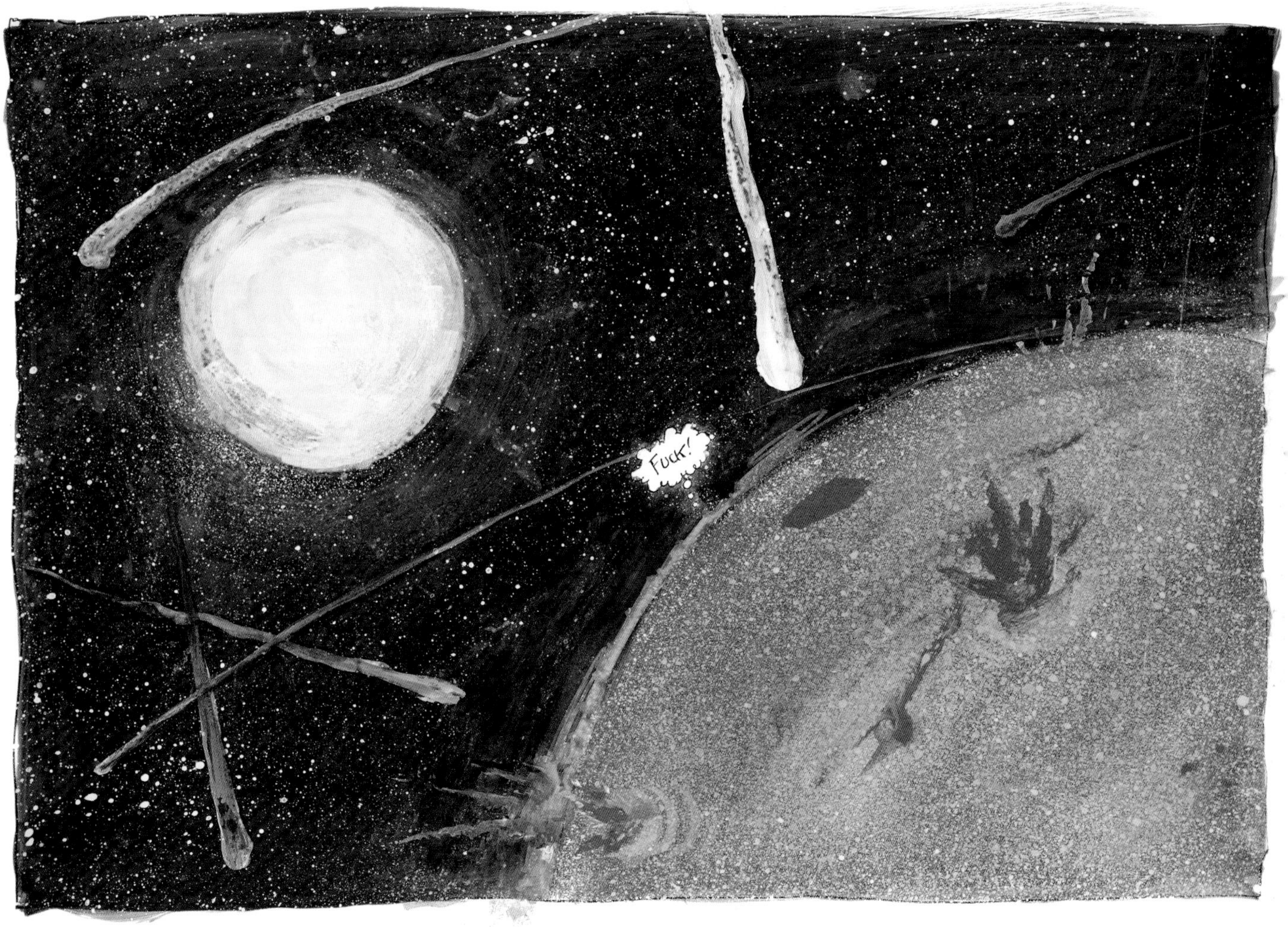
FUCK!

The Birth of Life

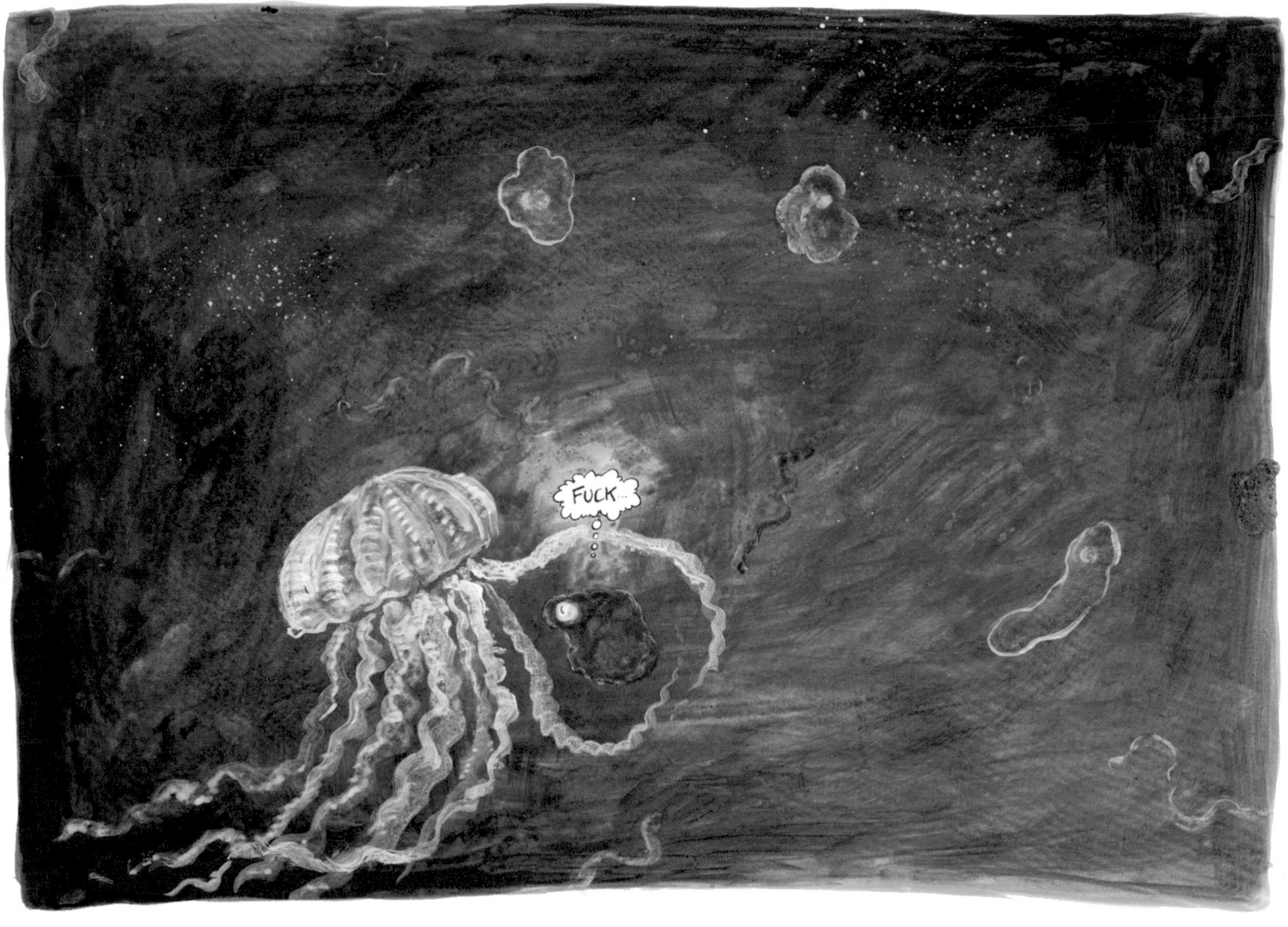
FUCK...

The Conquest of the Land

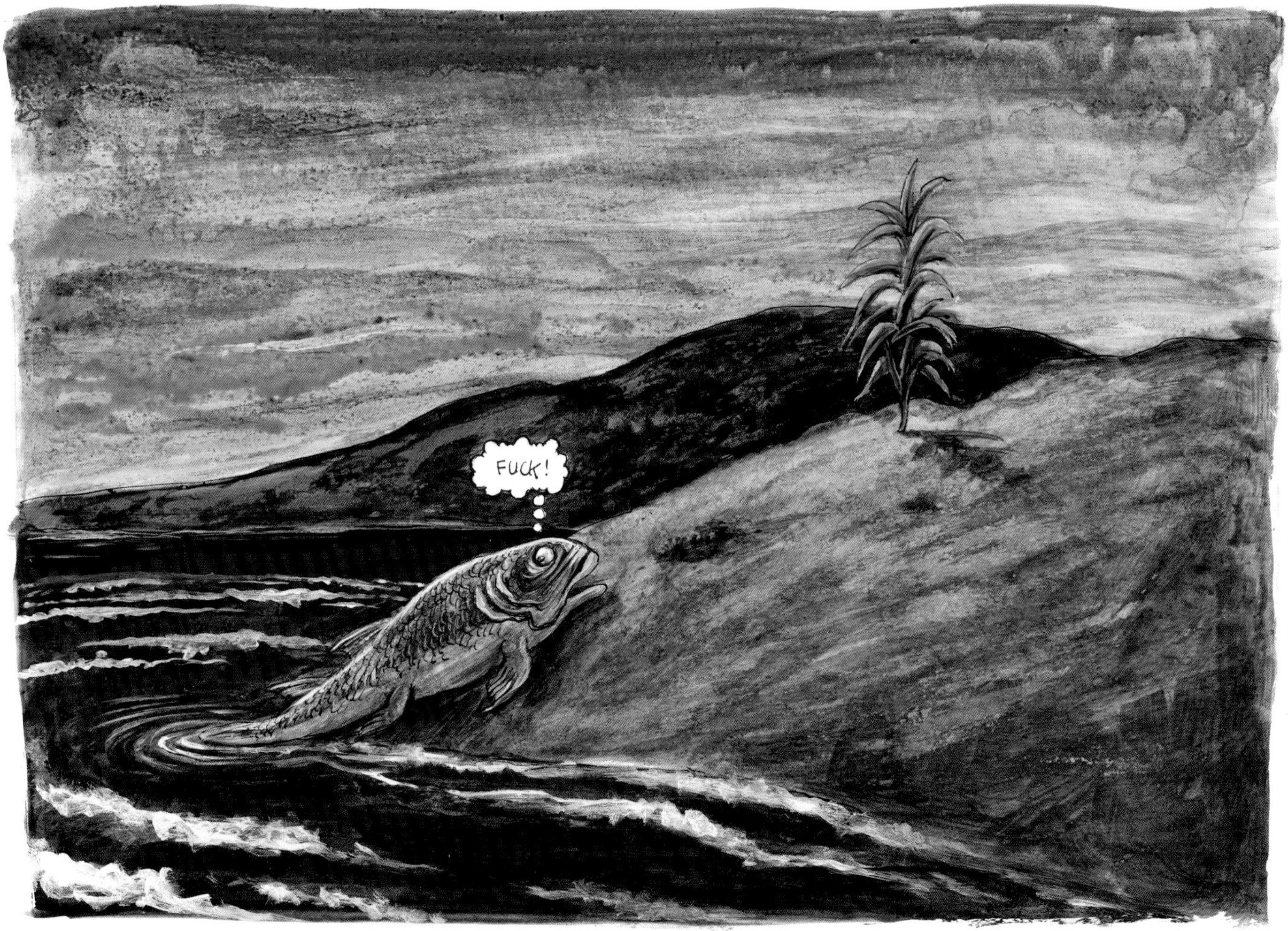
FUCK!

Dinosaurs Rule the Earth

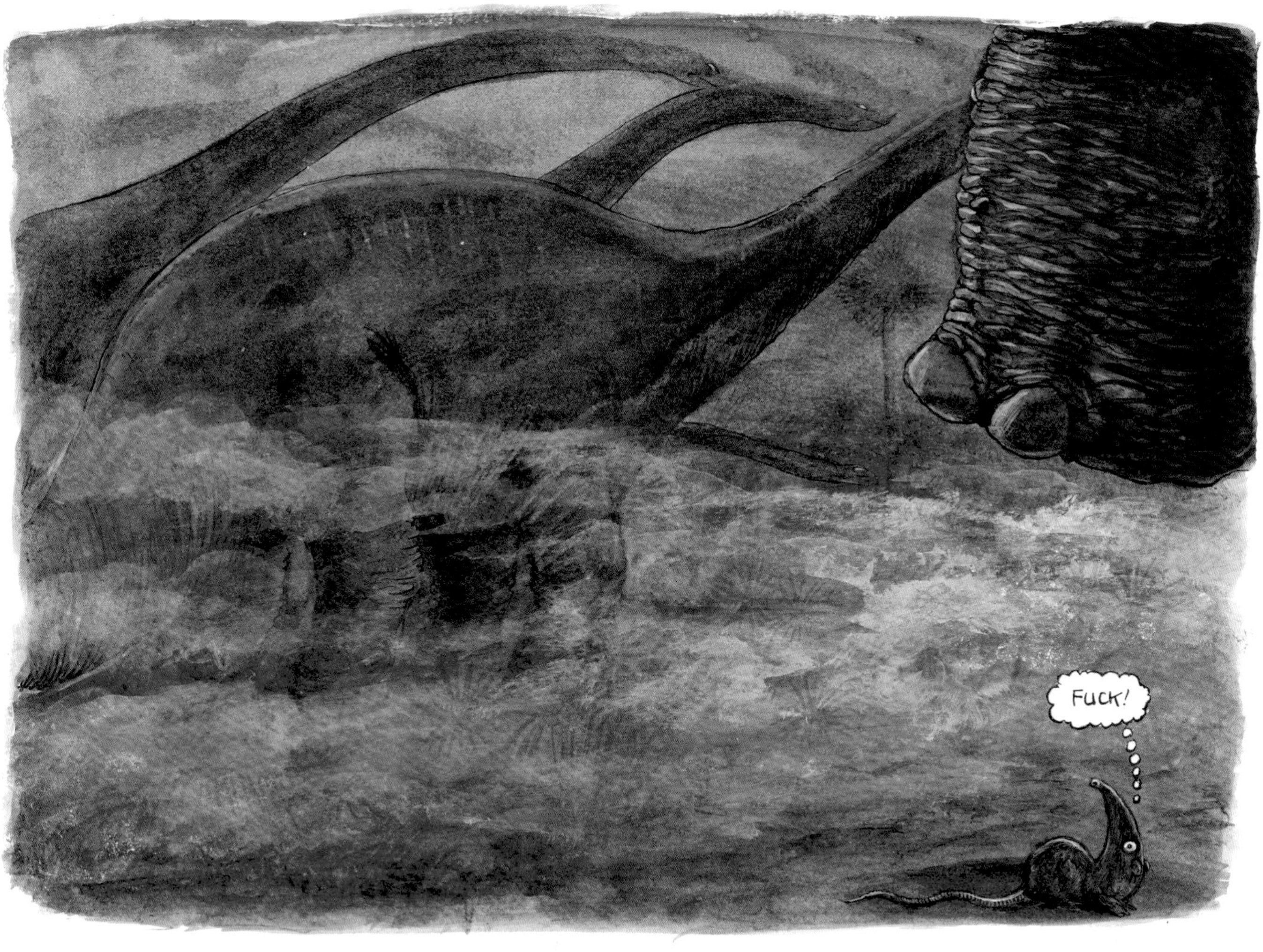
FUCK!

The Extinction of the Dinosaurs

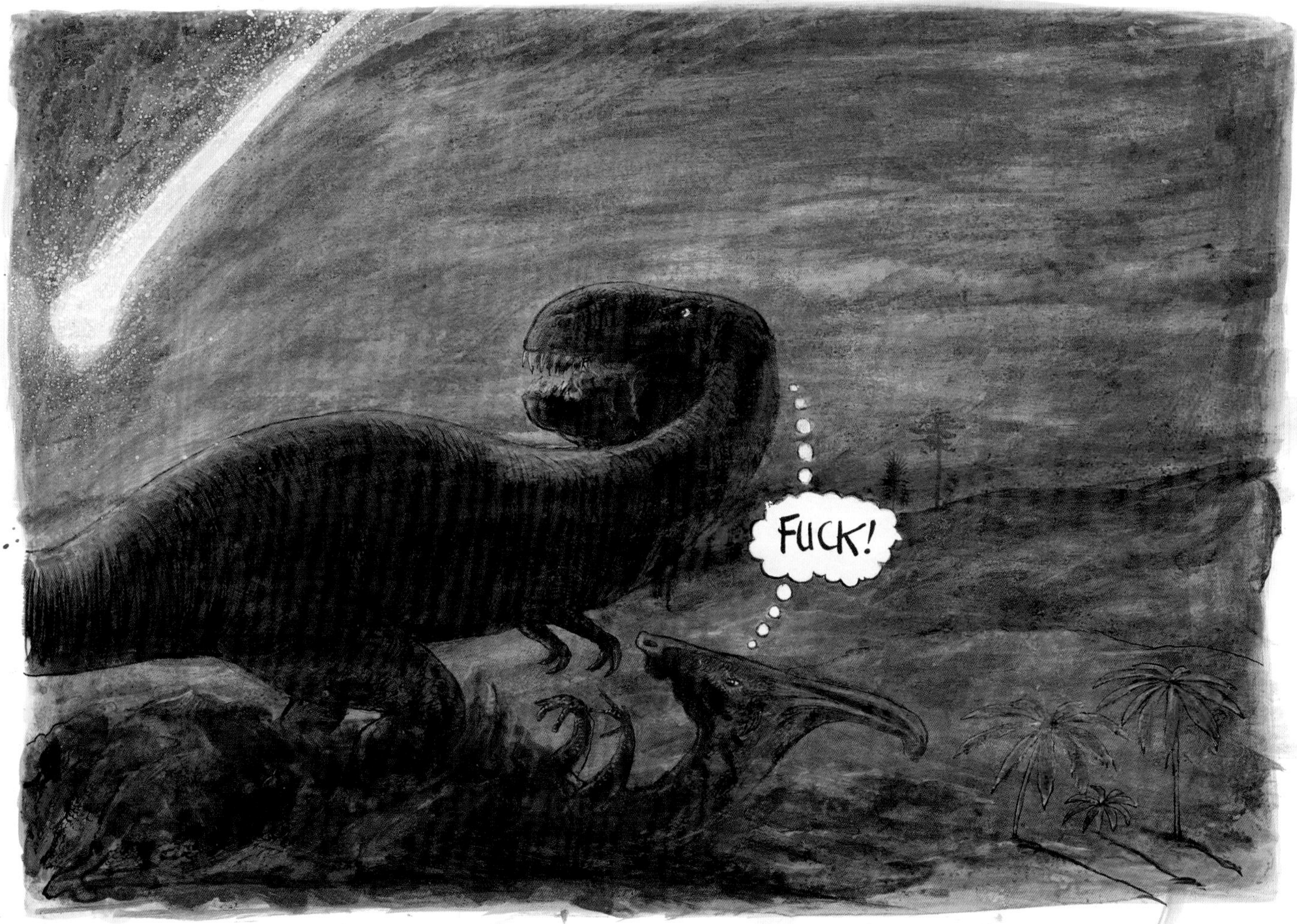
FUCK!

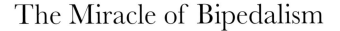

The Miracle of Bipedalism

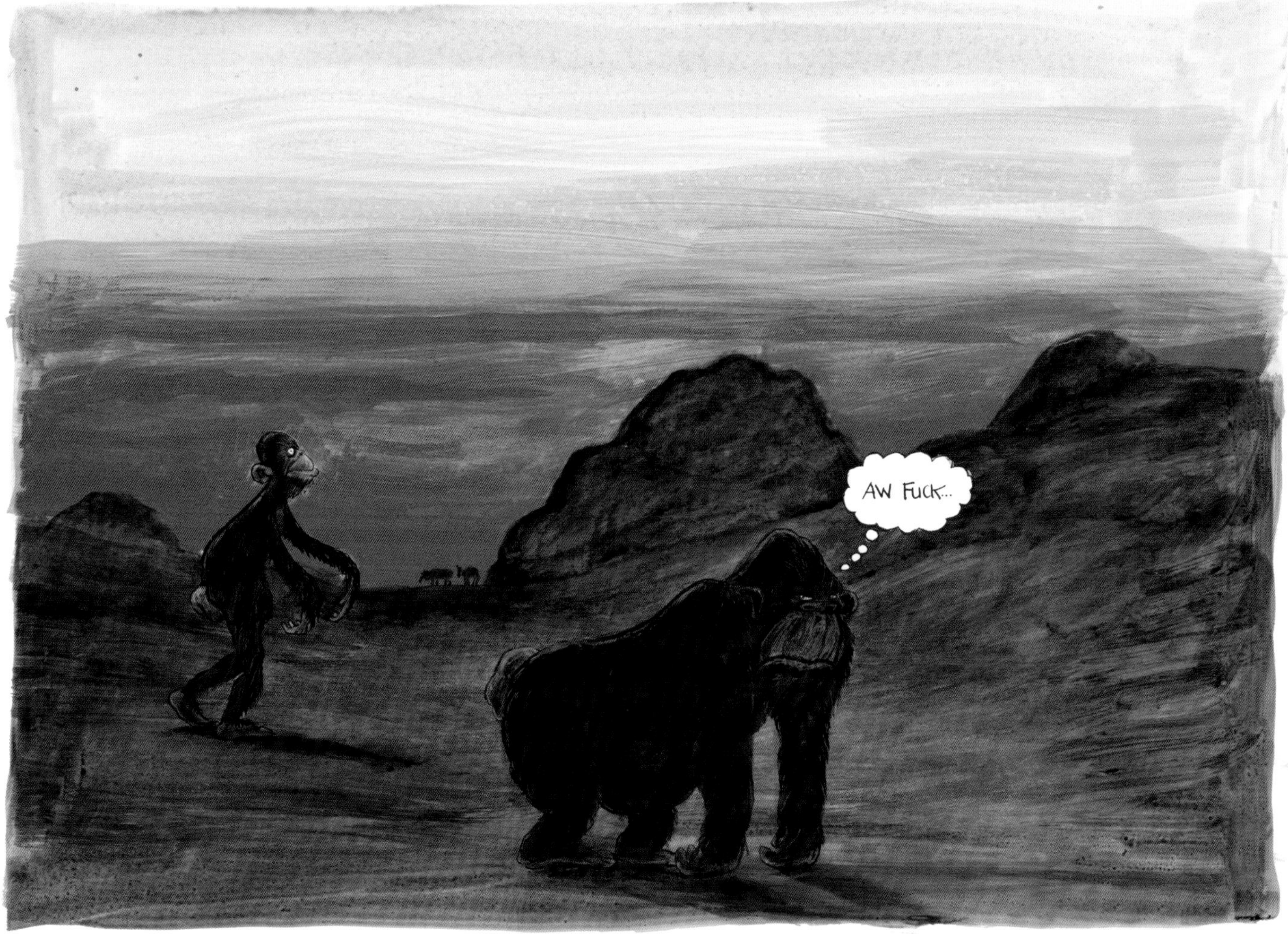
AW FUCK...

The Acquisition of Tools

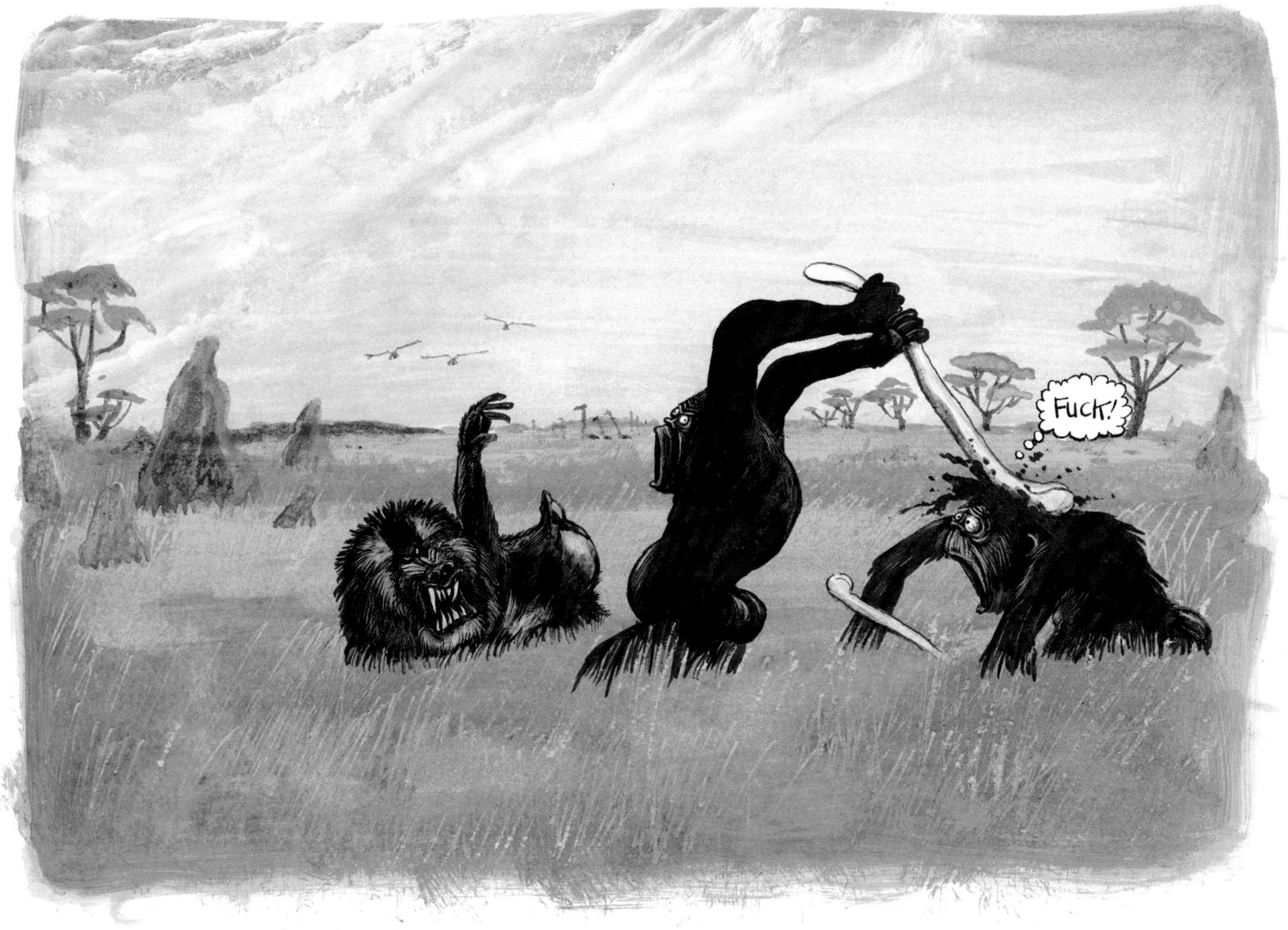
FUCK!

The Birth of Language

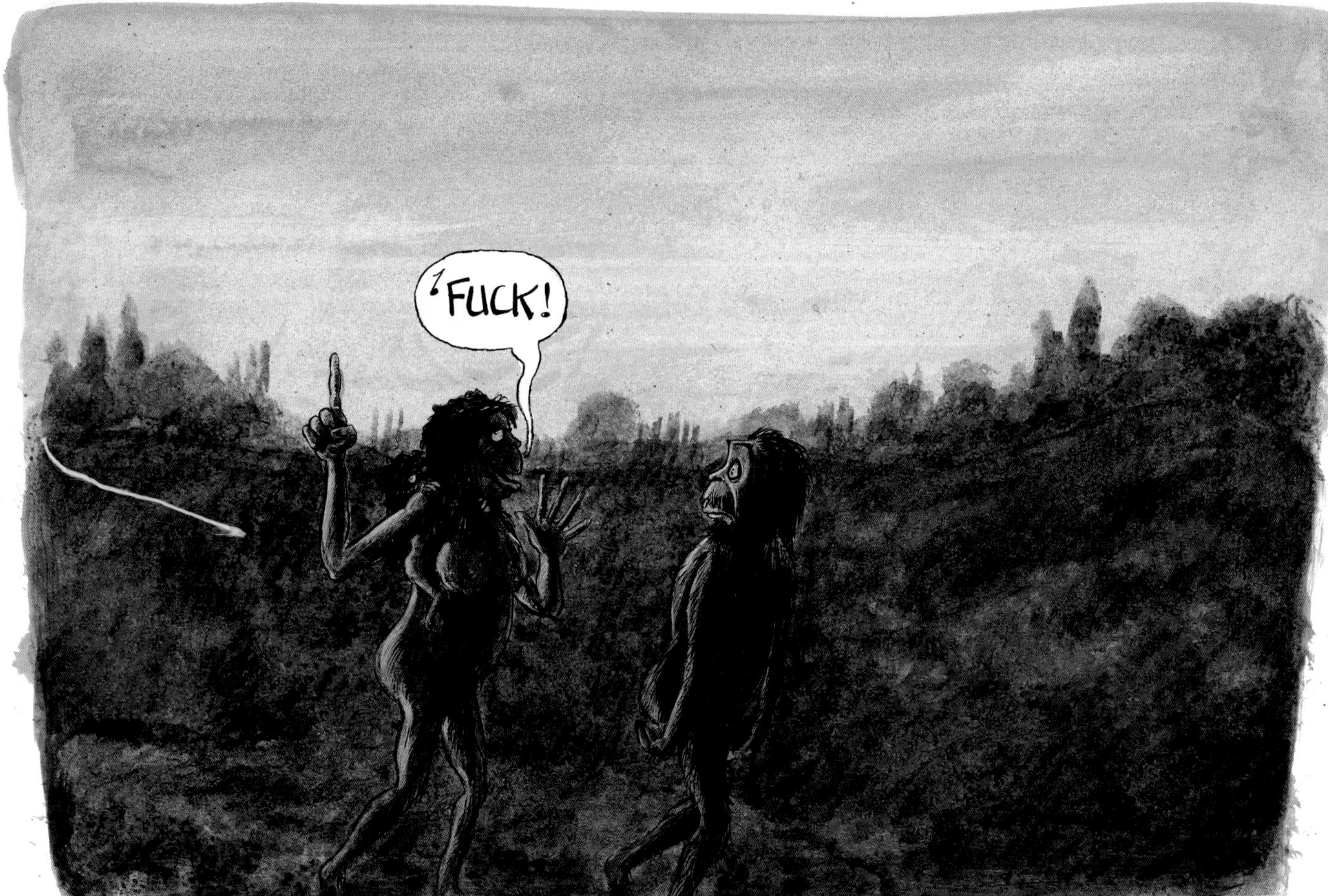
'FUCK!

The Neanderthals Die Out

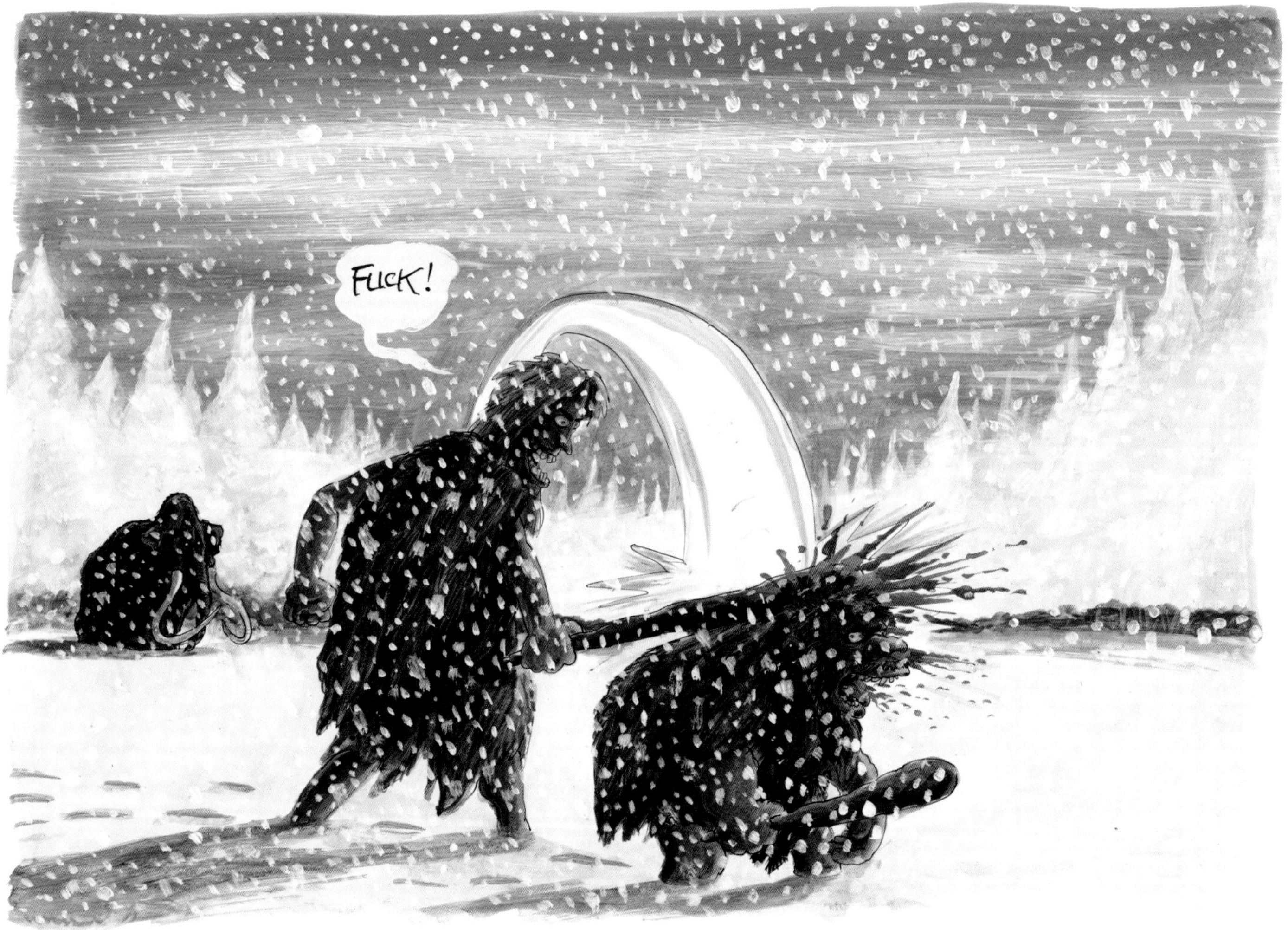
FUCK!

The Invention of the Wheel

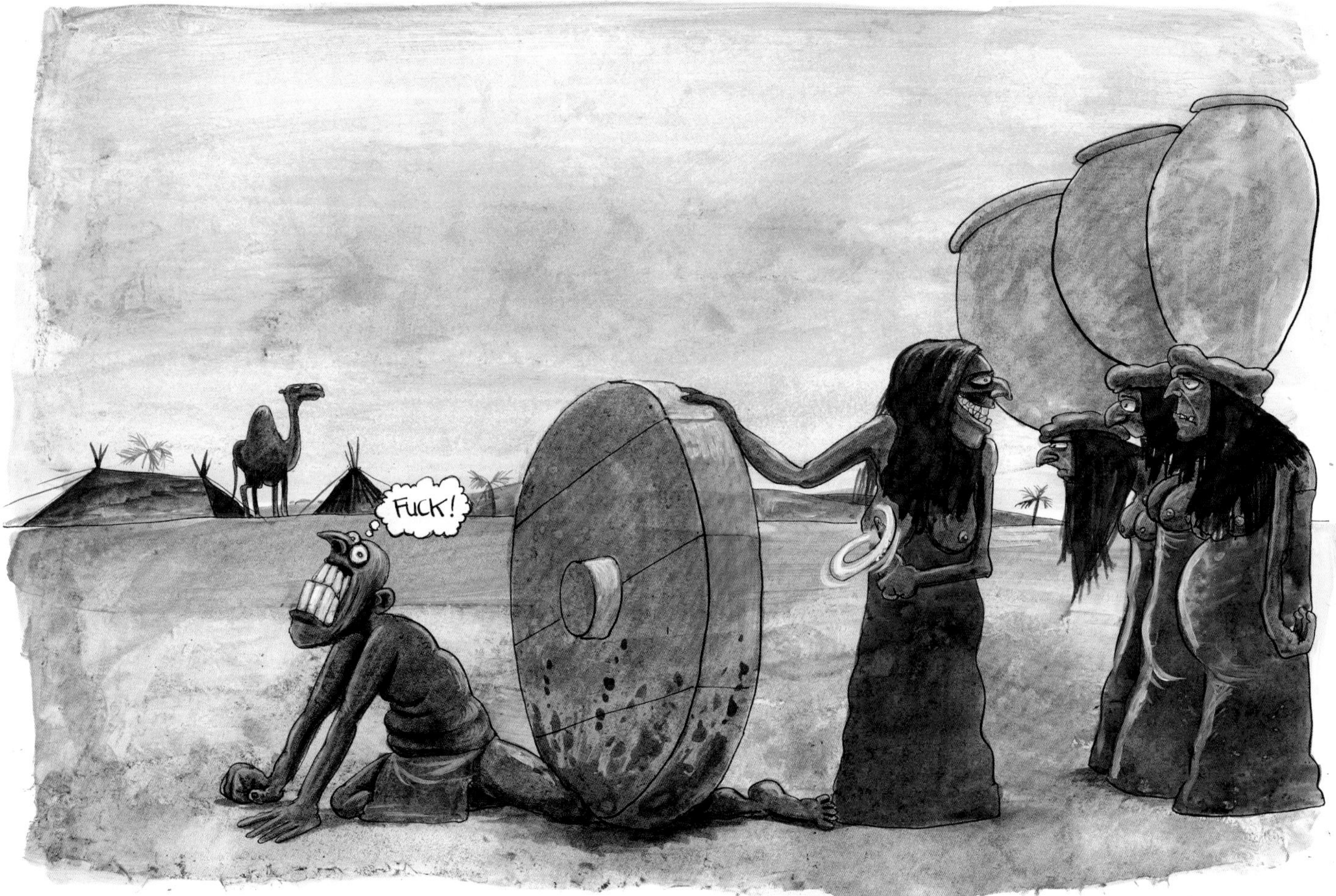
FUCK!

Agriculture

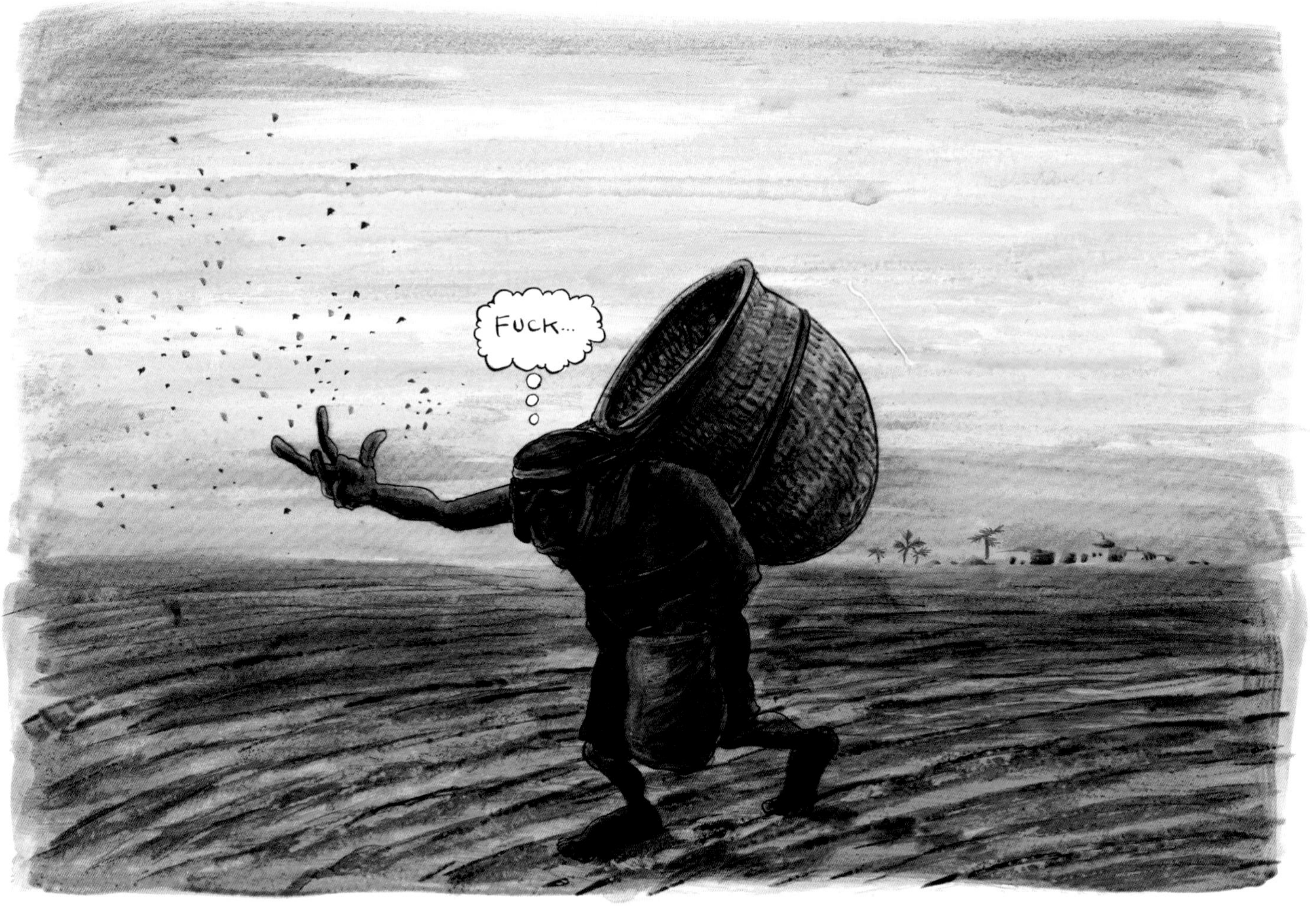
FUCK...

The Development of Writing

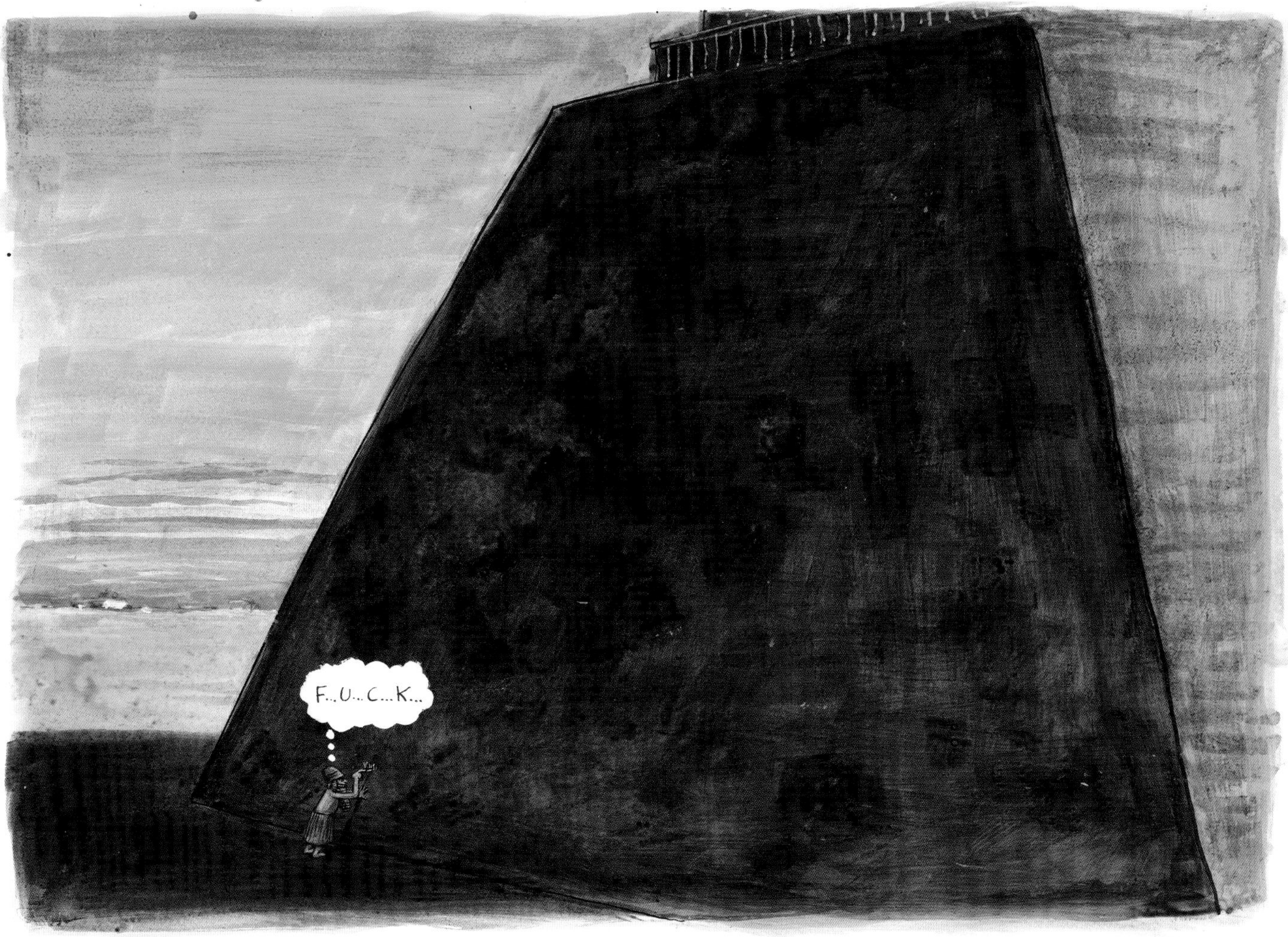
F...U...C...K...

The Siege of Troy

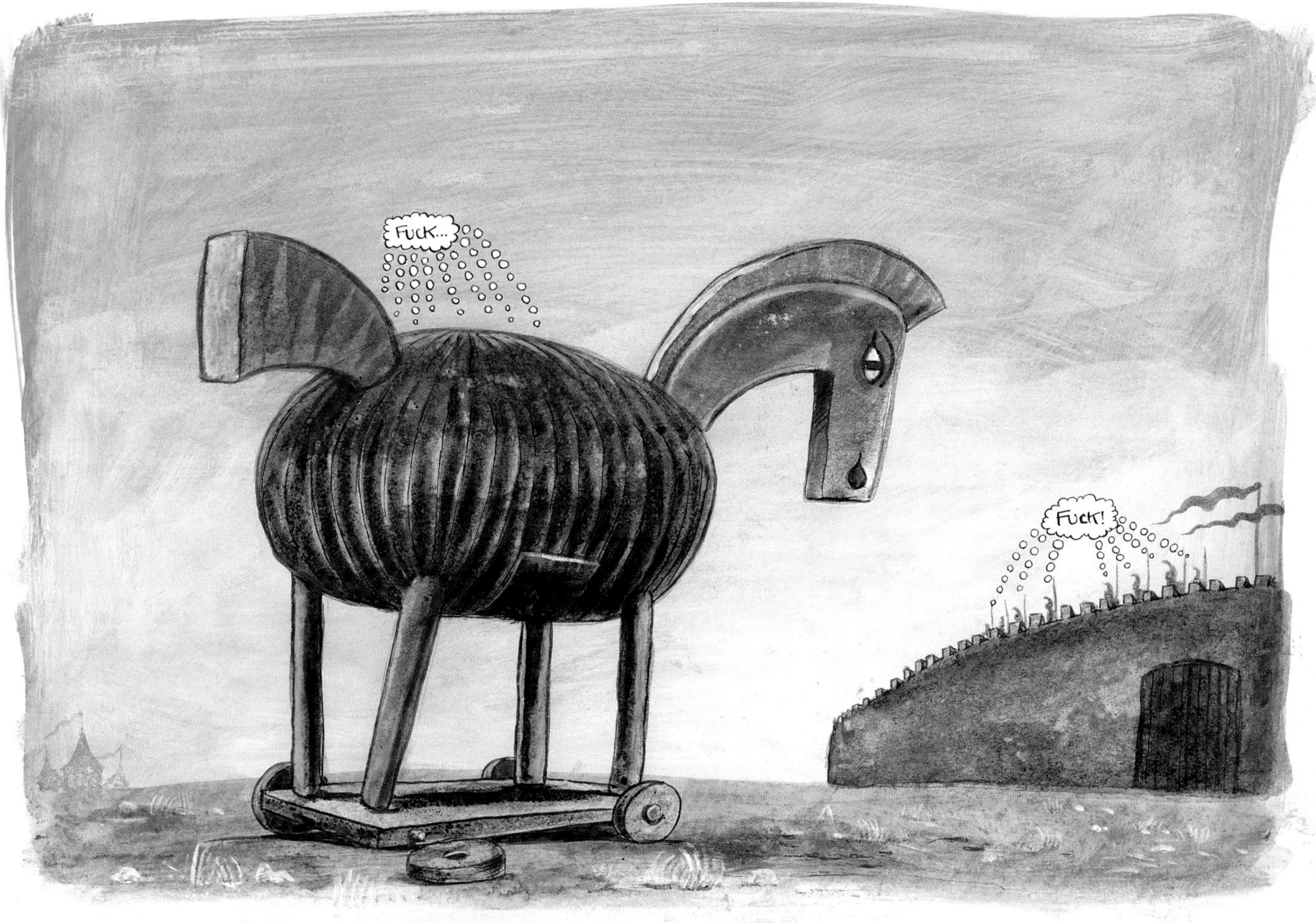
FUCK...
FUCK!

The Ten Commandments

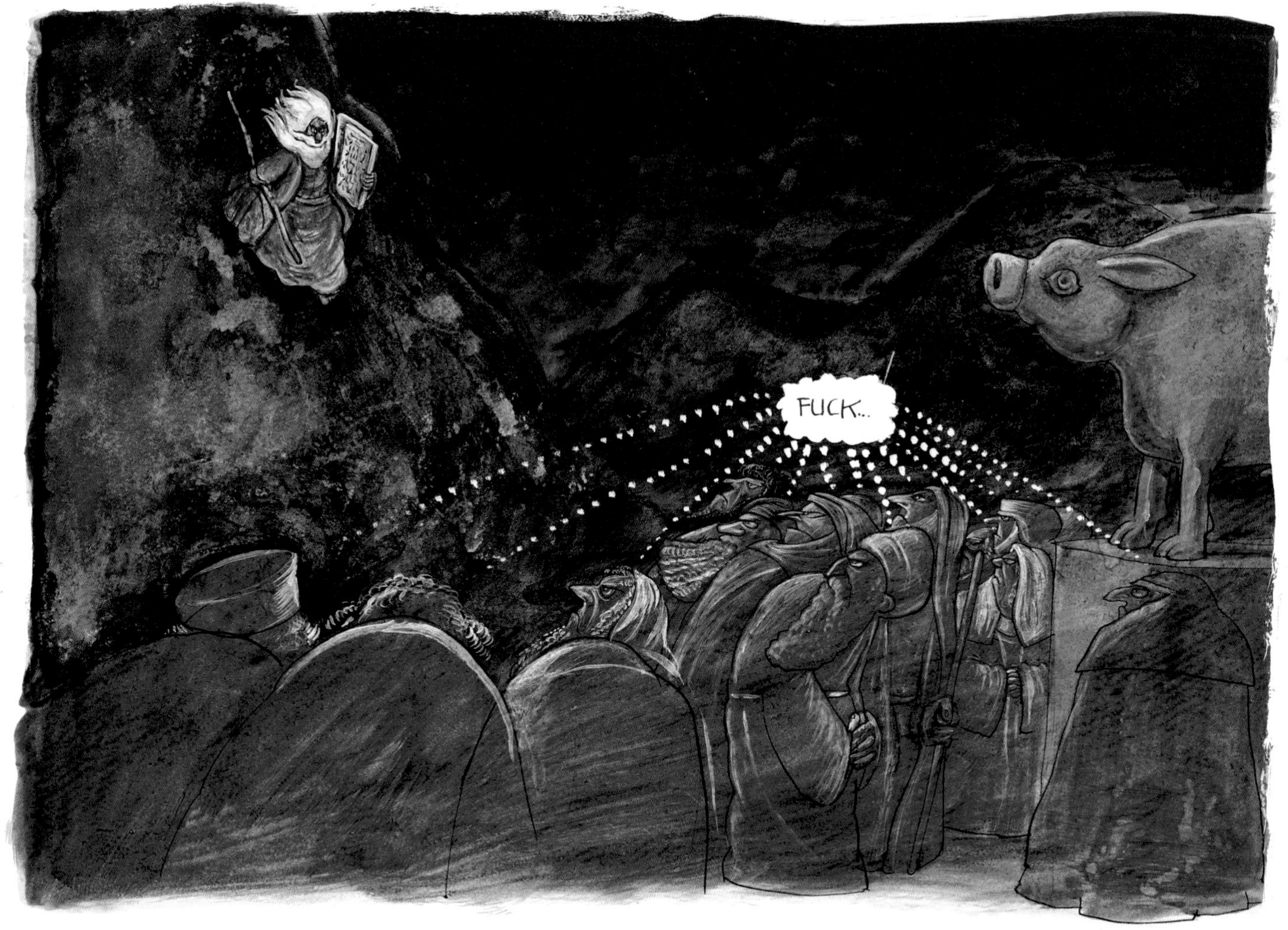
FUCK...

Athenian Philosophy

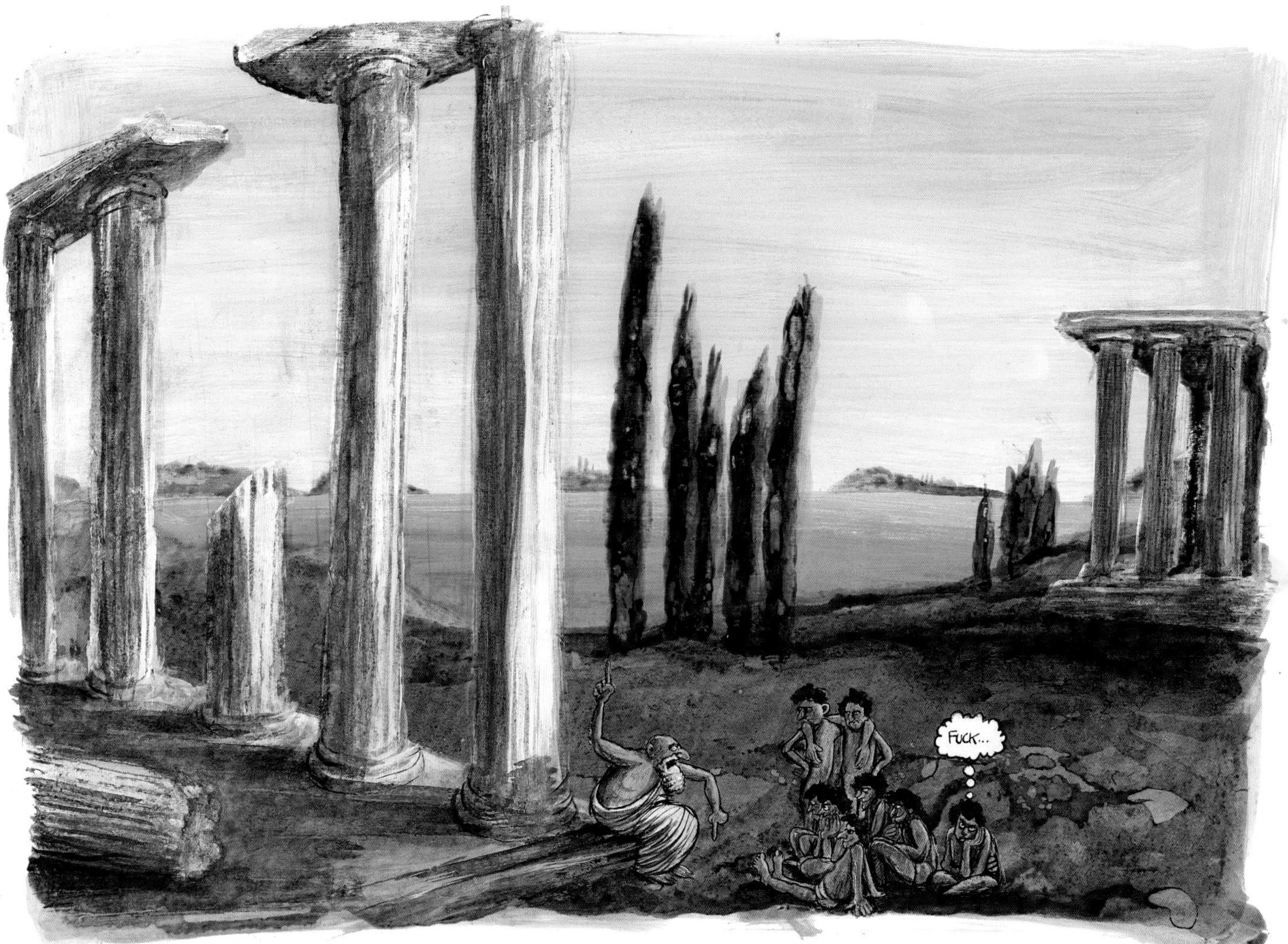
FUCK...

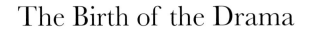

The Birth of the Drama

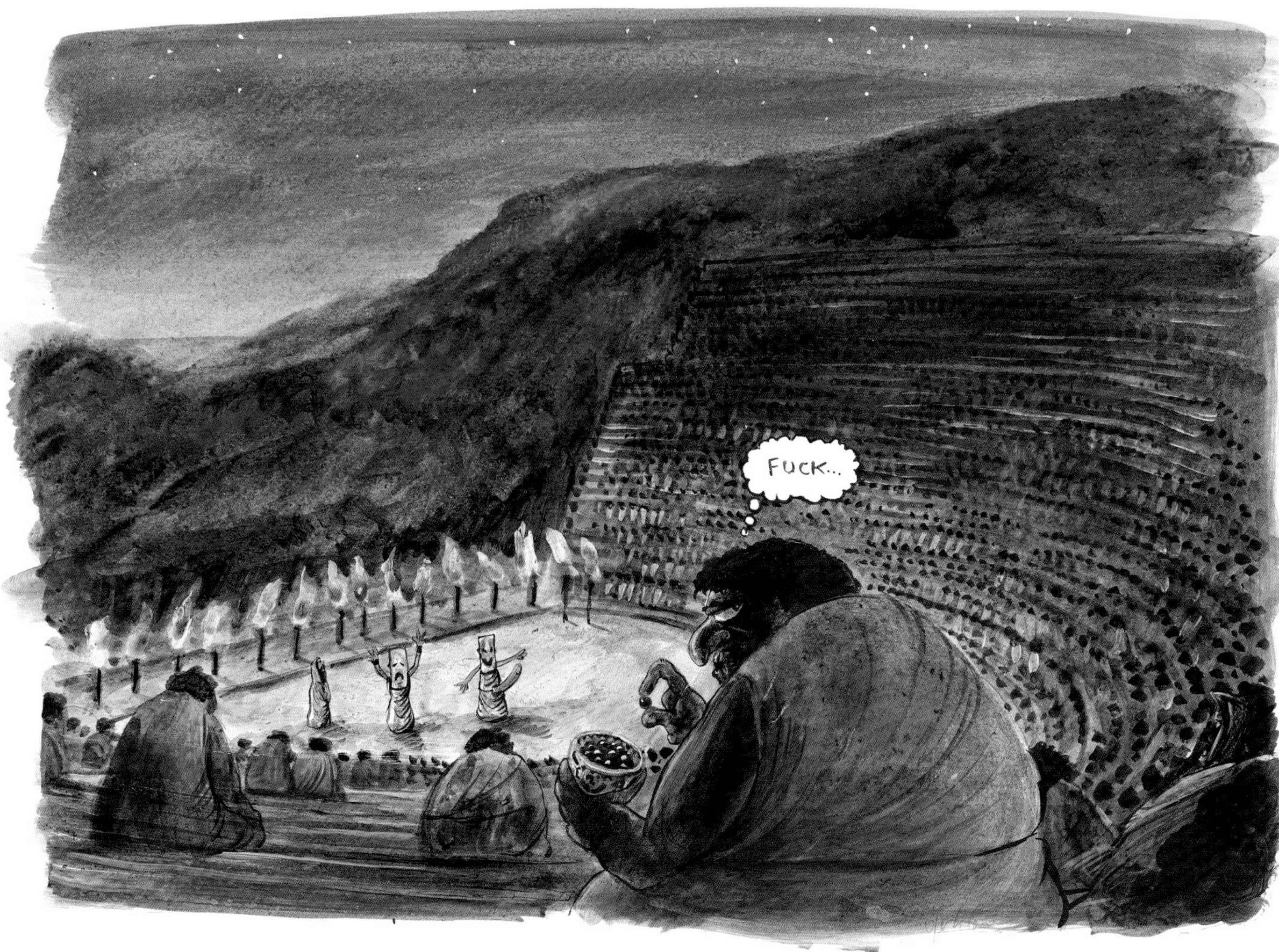
FUCK...

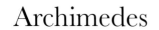

Archimedes

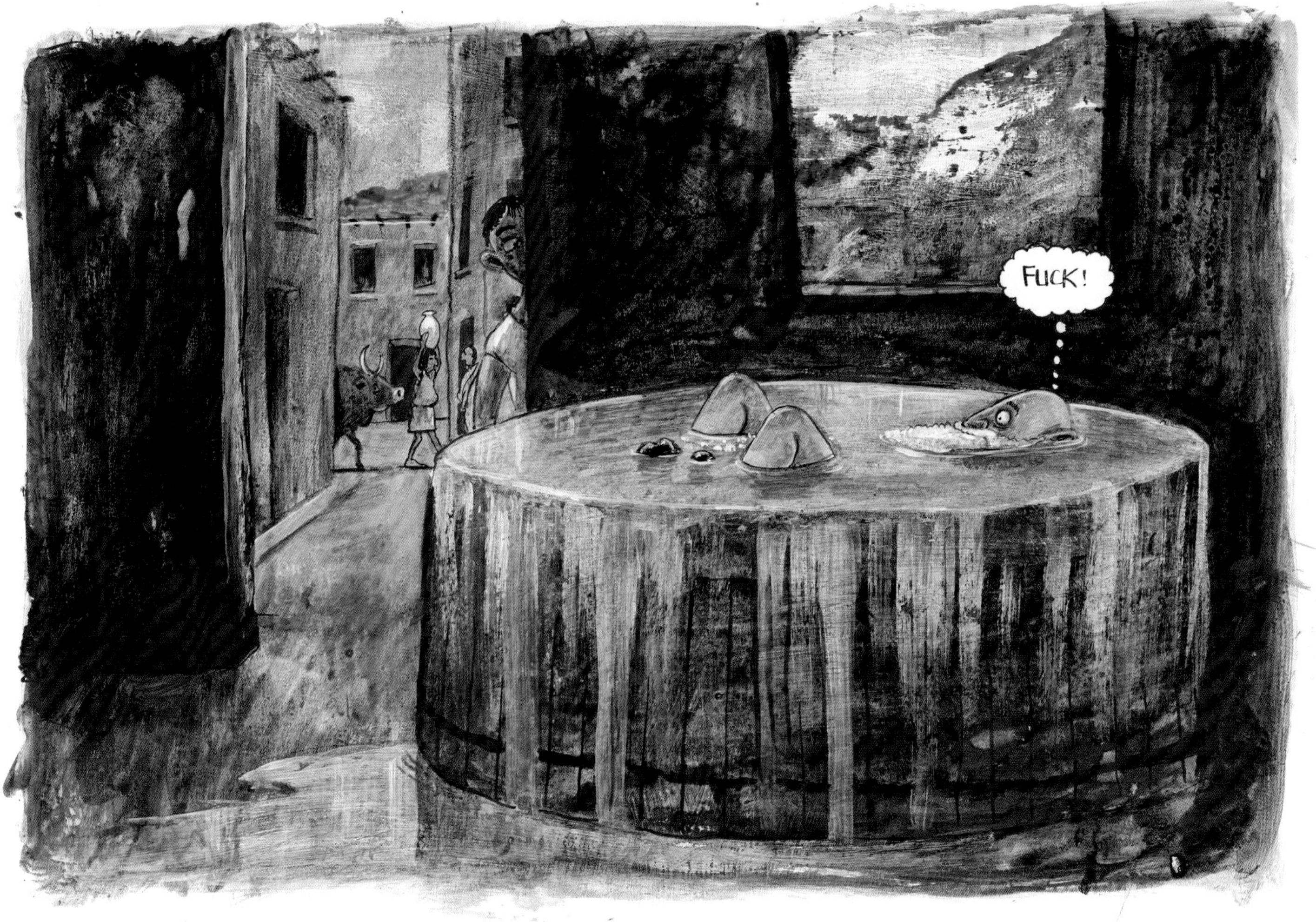
FUCK!

The Adoration of the Magi

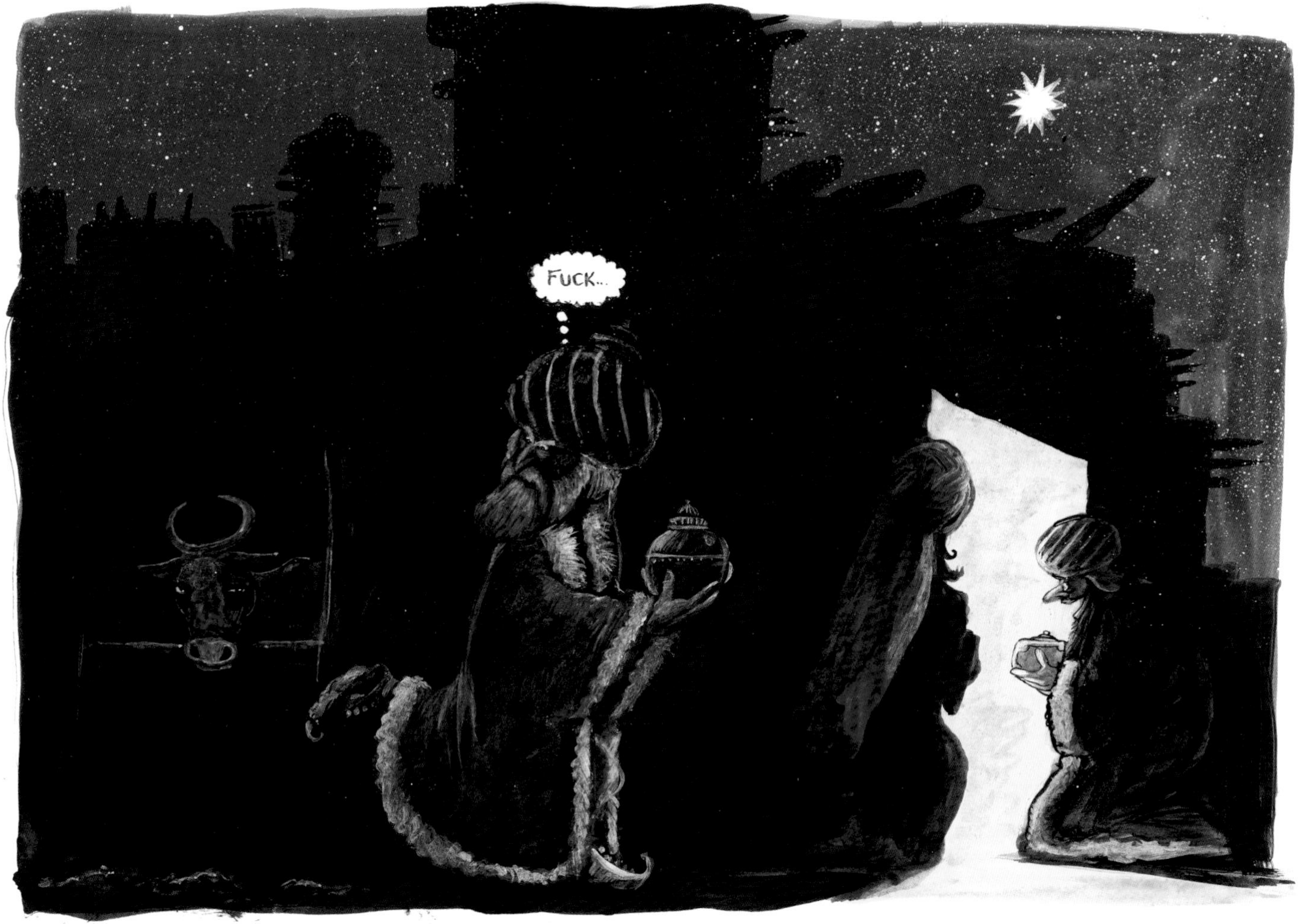
FUCK...

The Passion of our Lord

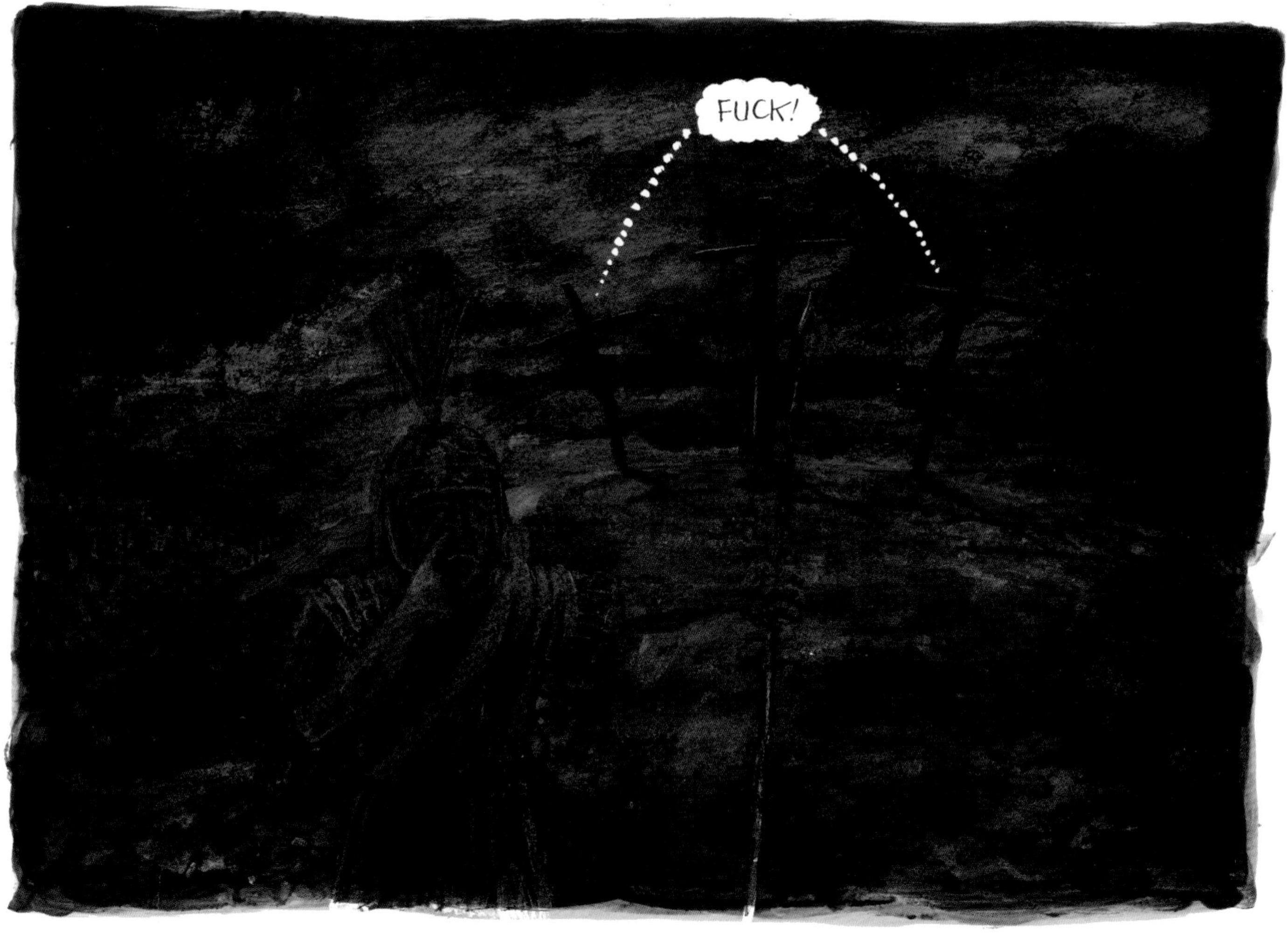
FUCK!

The Decline and Fall of the Roman Empire

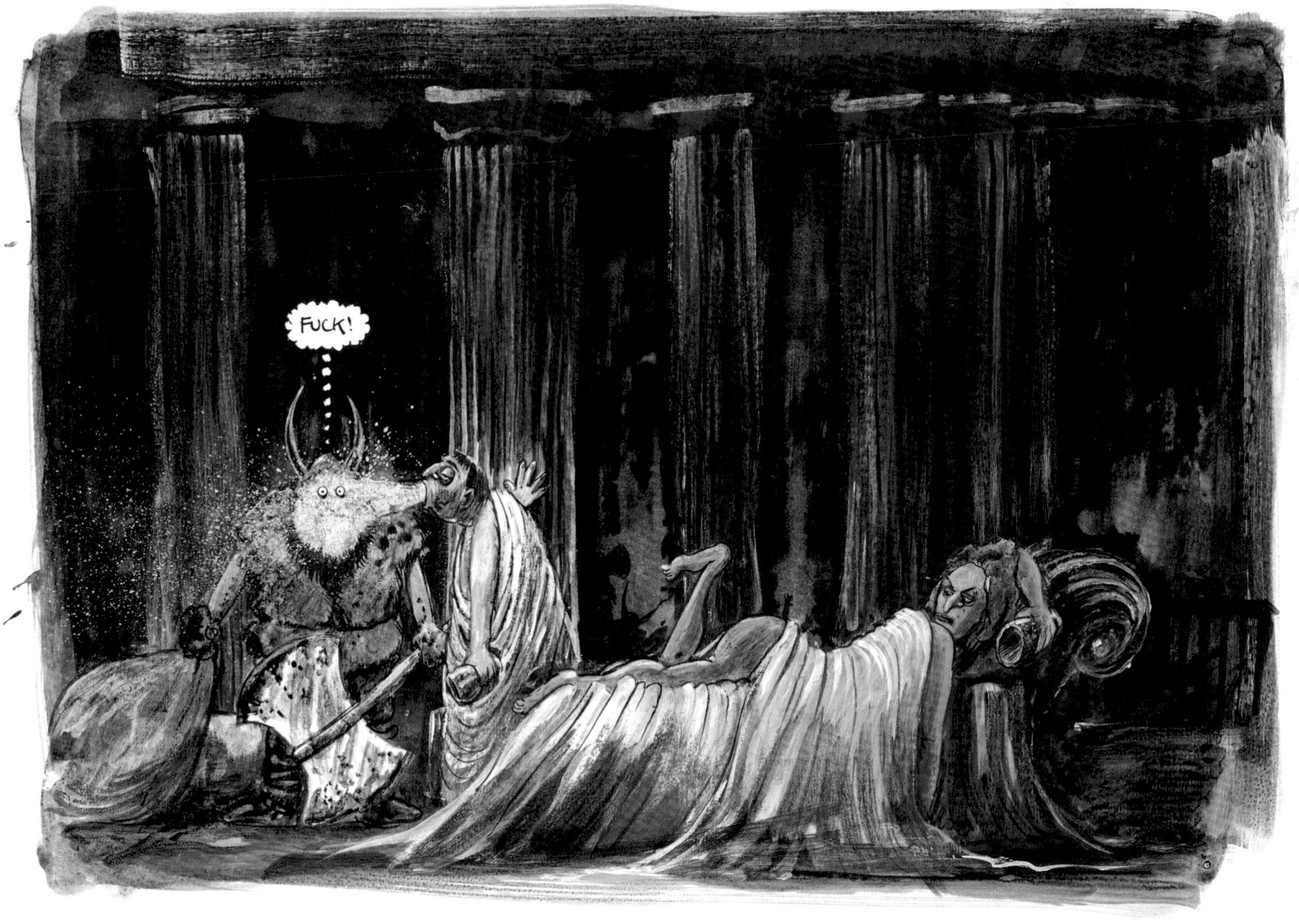
FUCK!

Monasticism Keeps Learning Alive through the Dark Ages

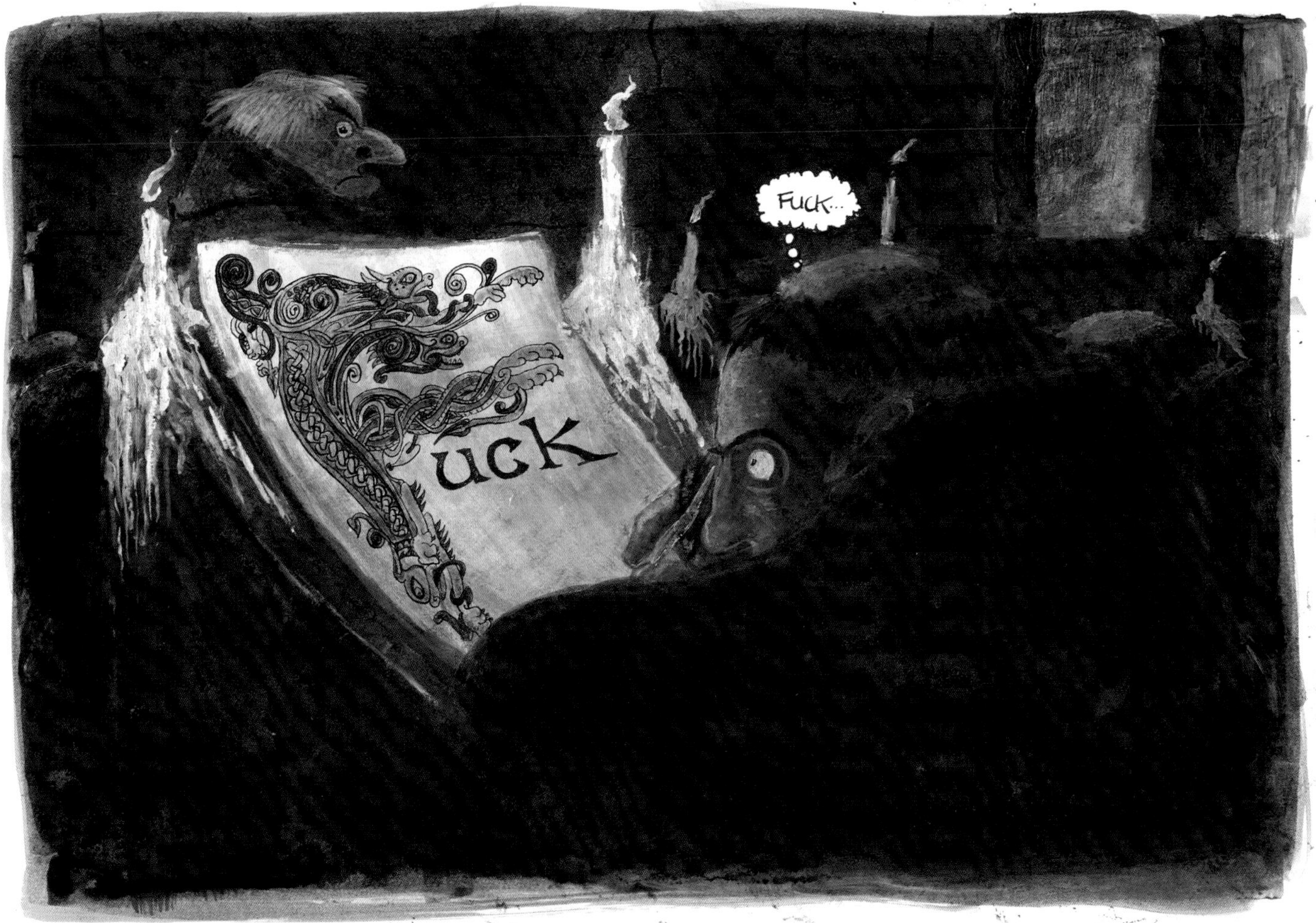
UCK
FUCK...

The Vikings

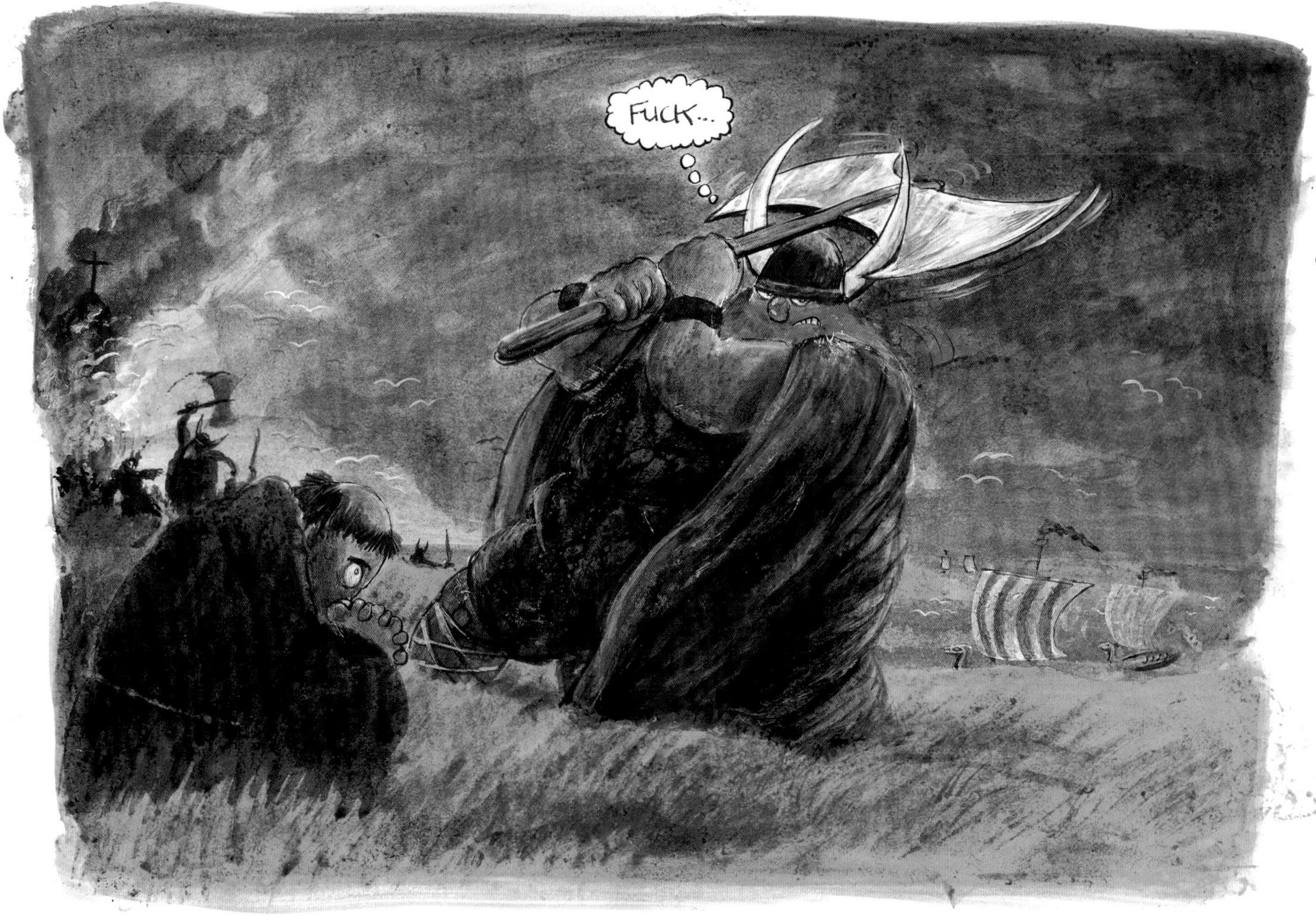
FUCK...

The Age of Chivalry

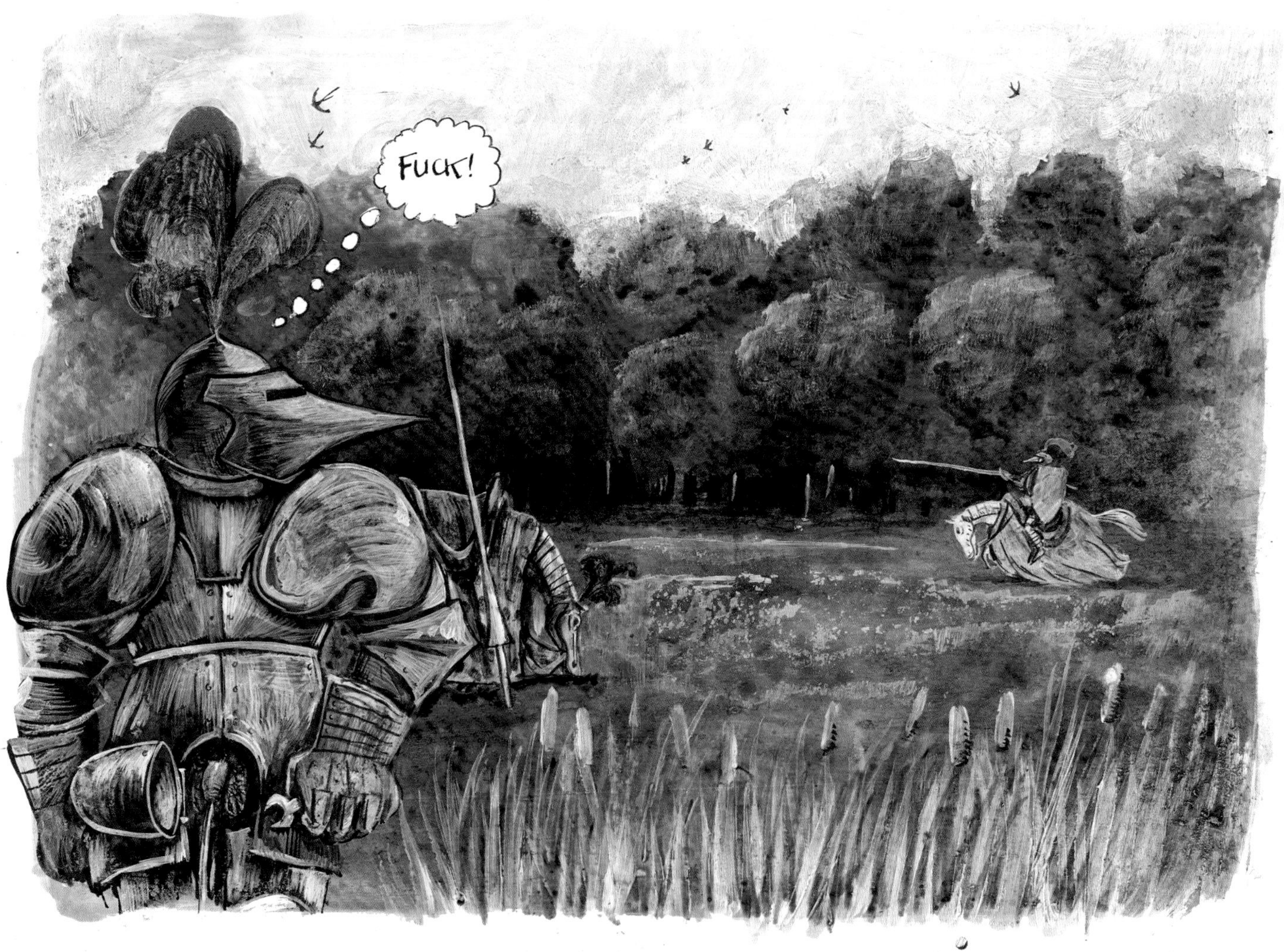
FUCK!

The Black Death

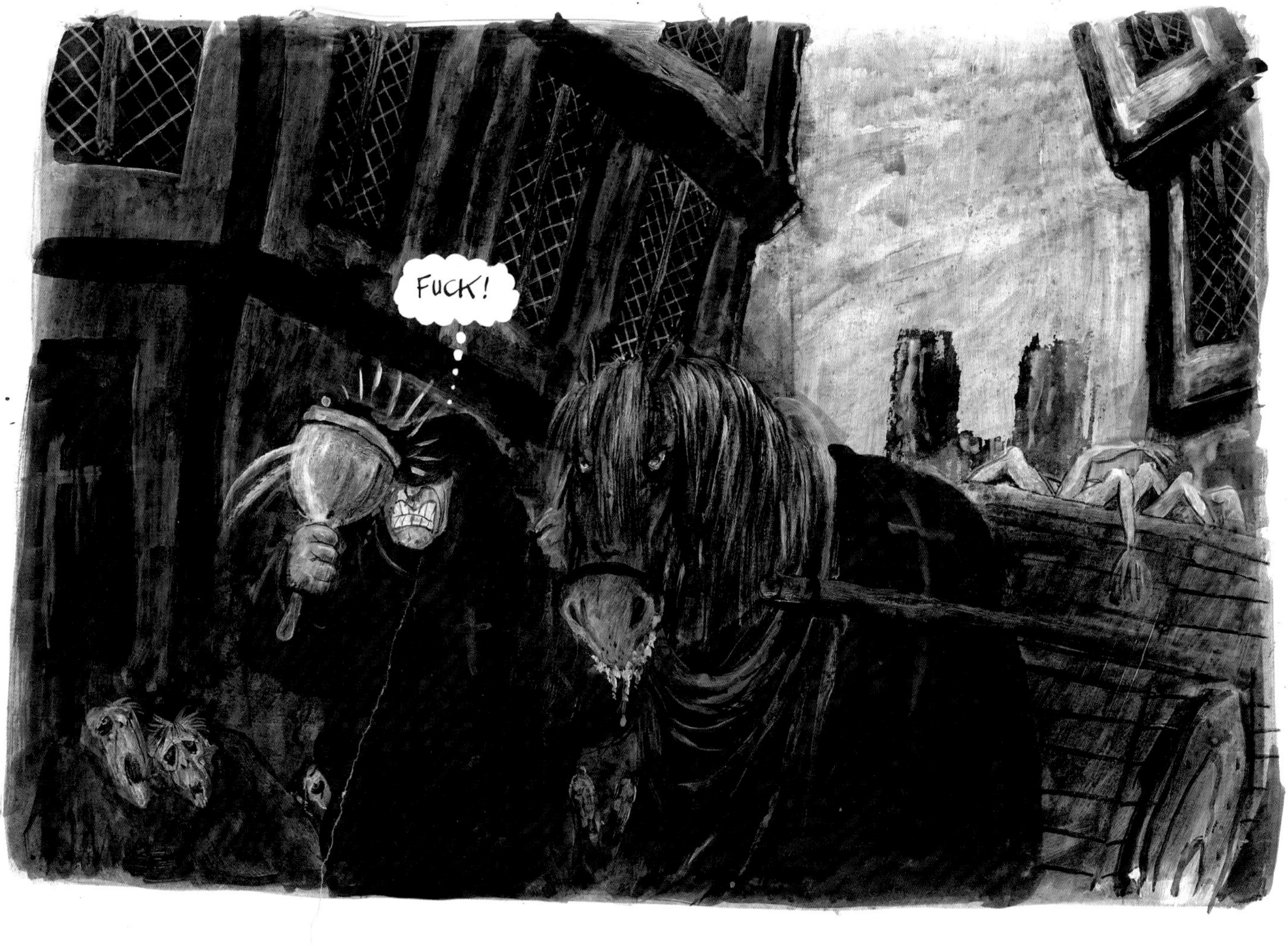
FUCK!

Chaucer's Canterbury Pilgrims

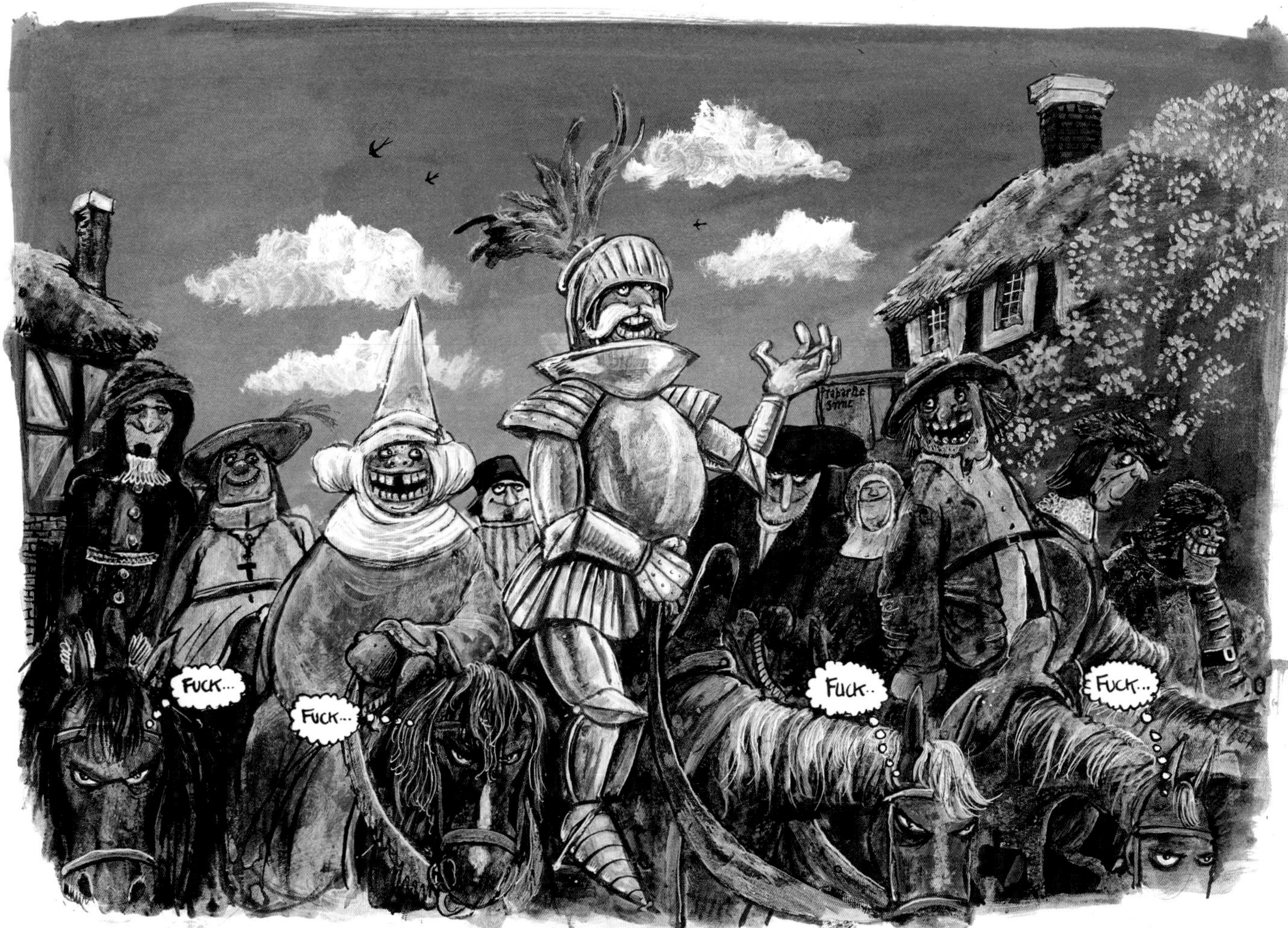
FUCK...
FUCK...
FUCK..
FUCK...

The Invention of Printing

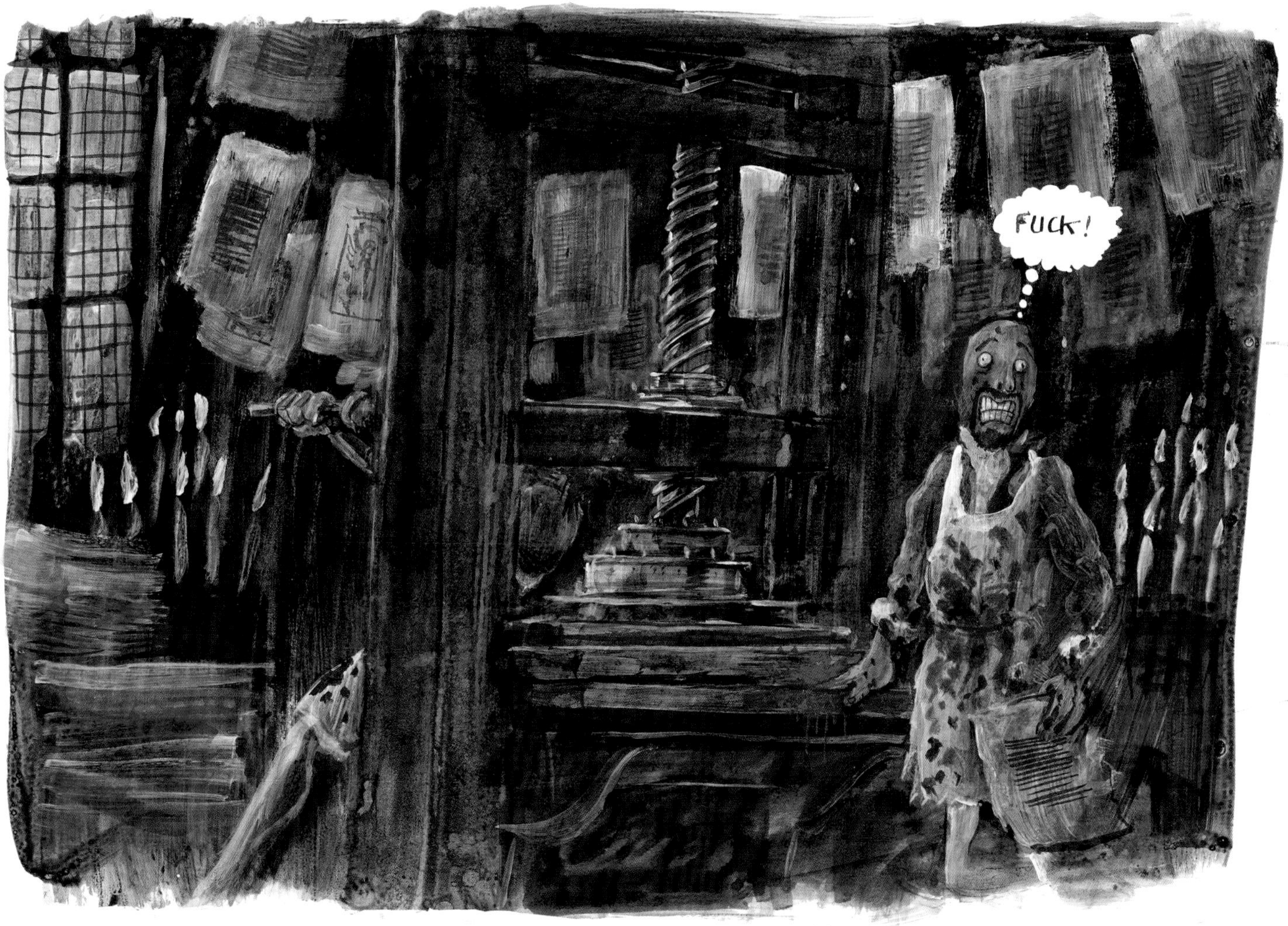
FUCK!

The Discovery of the New World

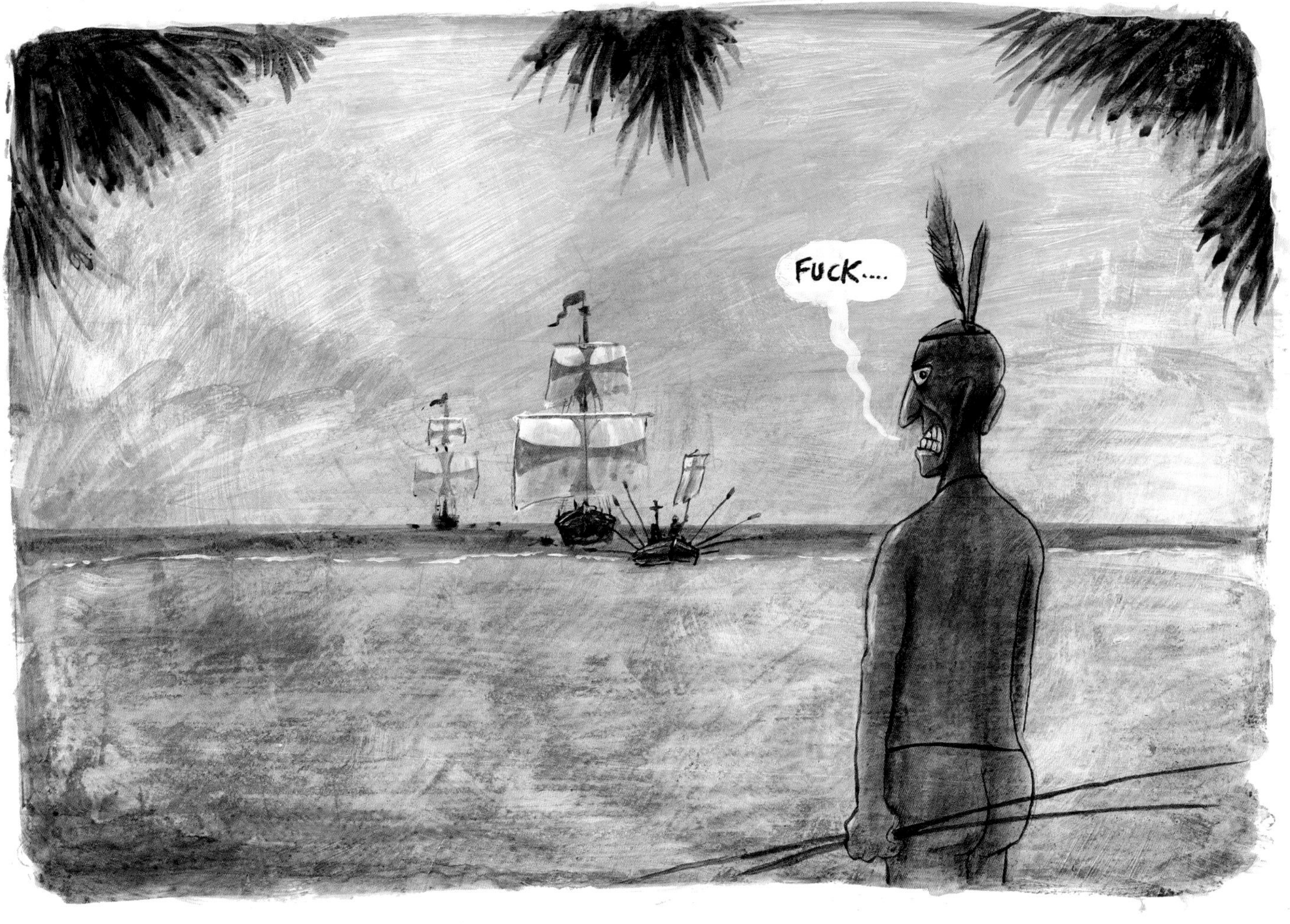
FUCK....

The High Renaissance

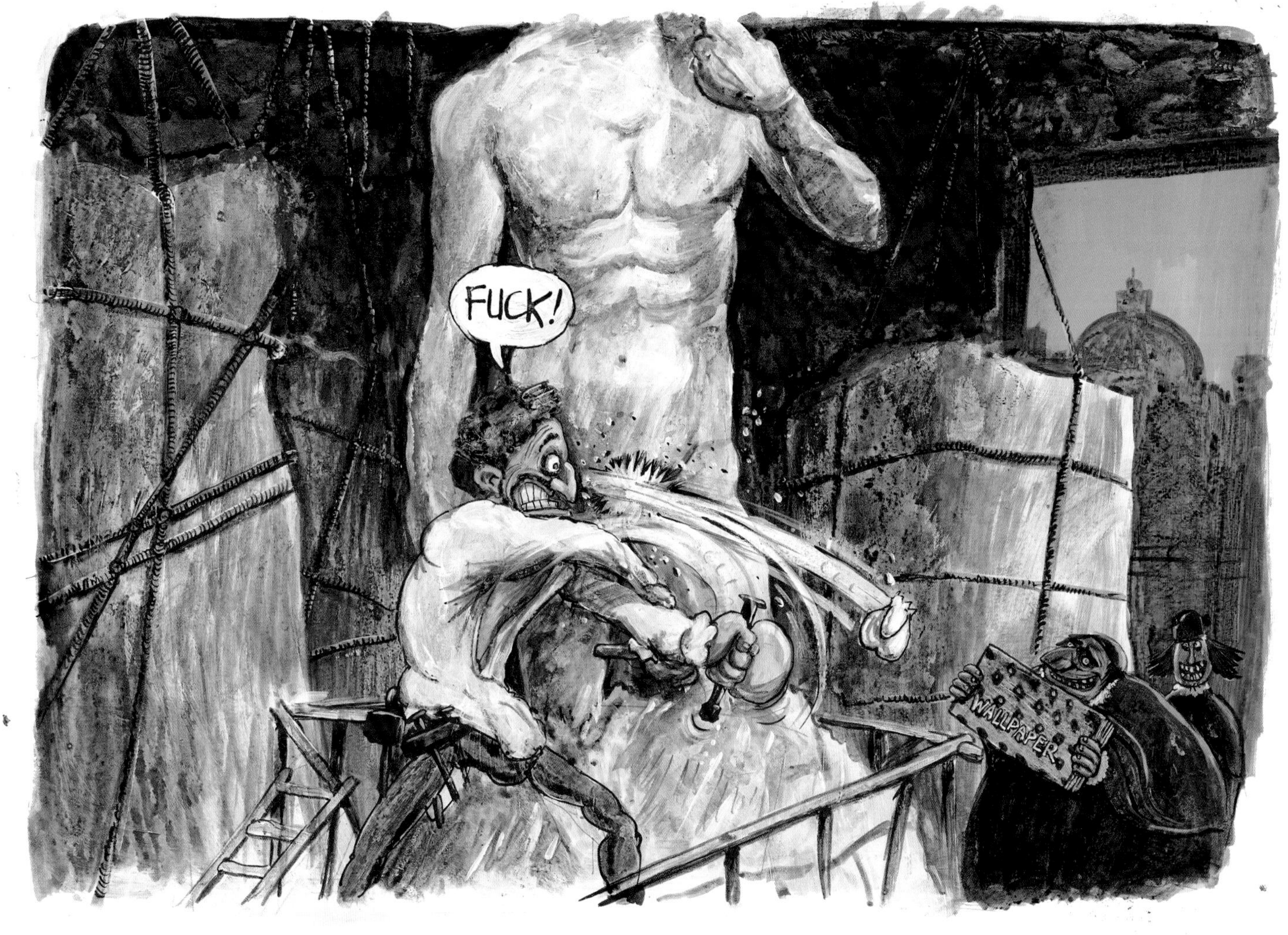
FUCK!
WALLPAPER

Luther Launches the Reformation

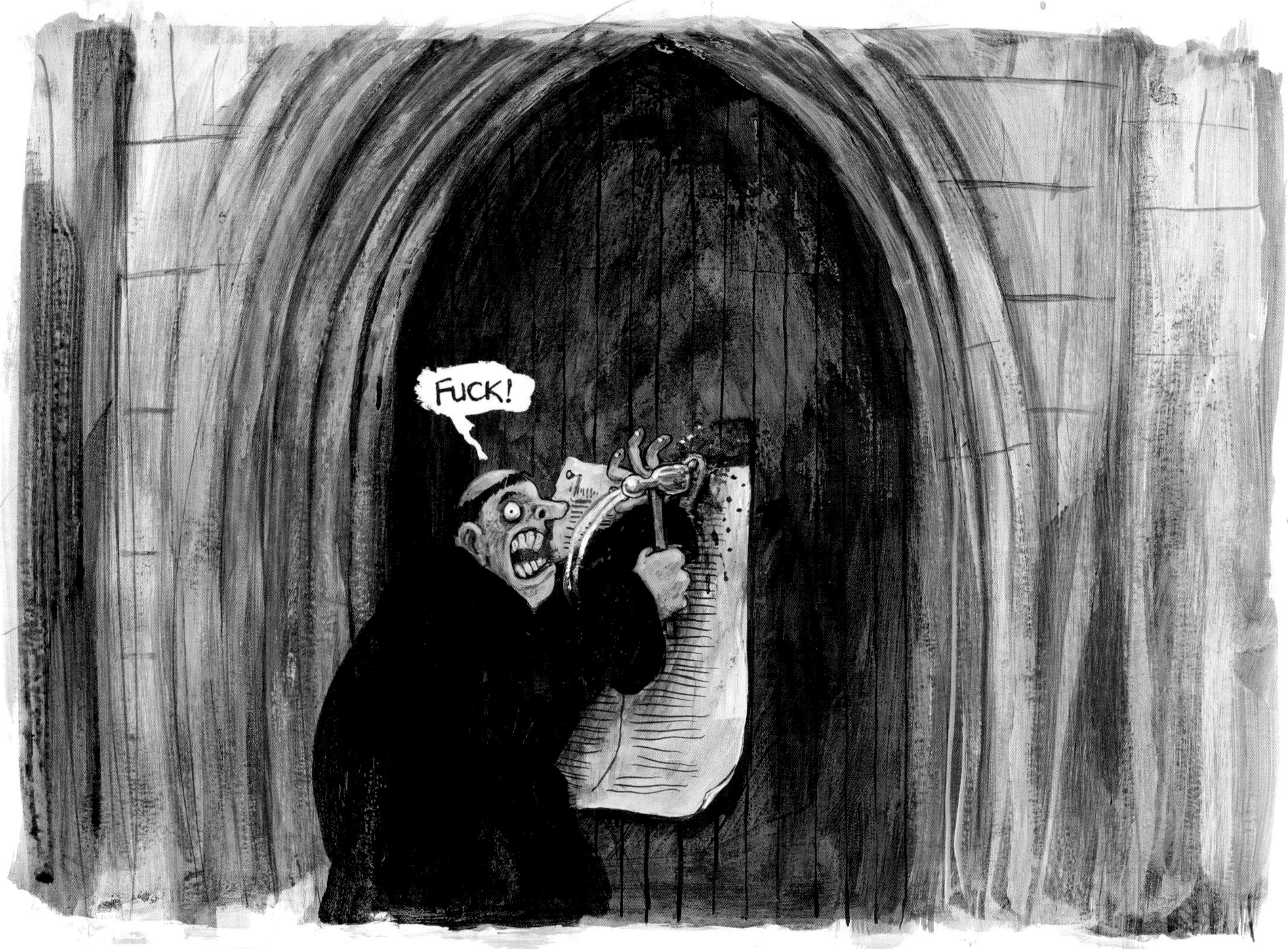
FUCK!

The Shakespearean Theater

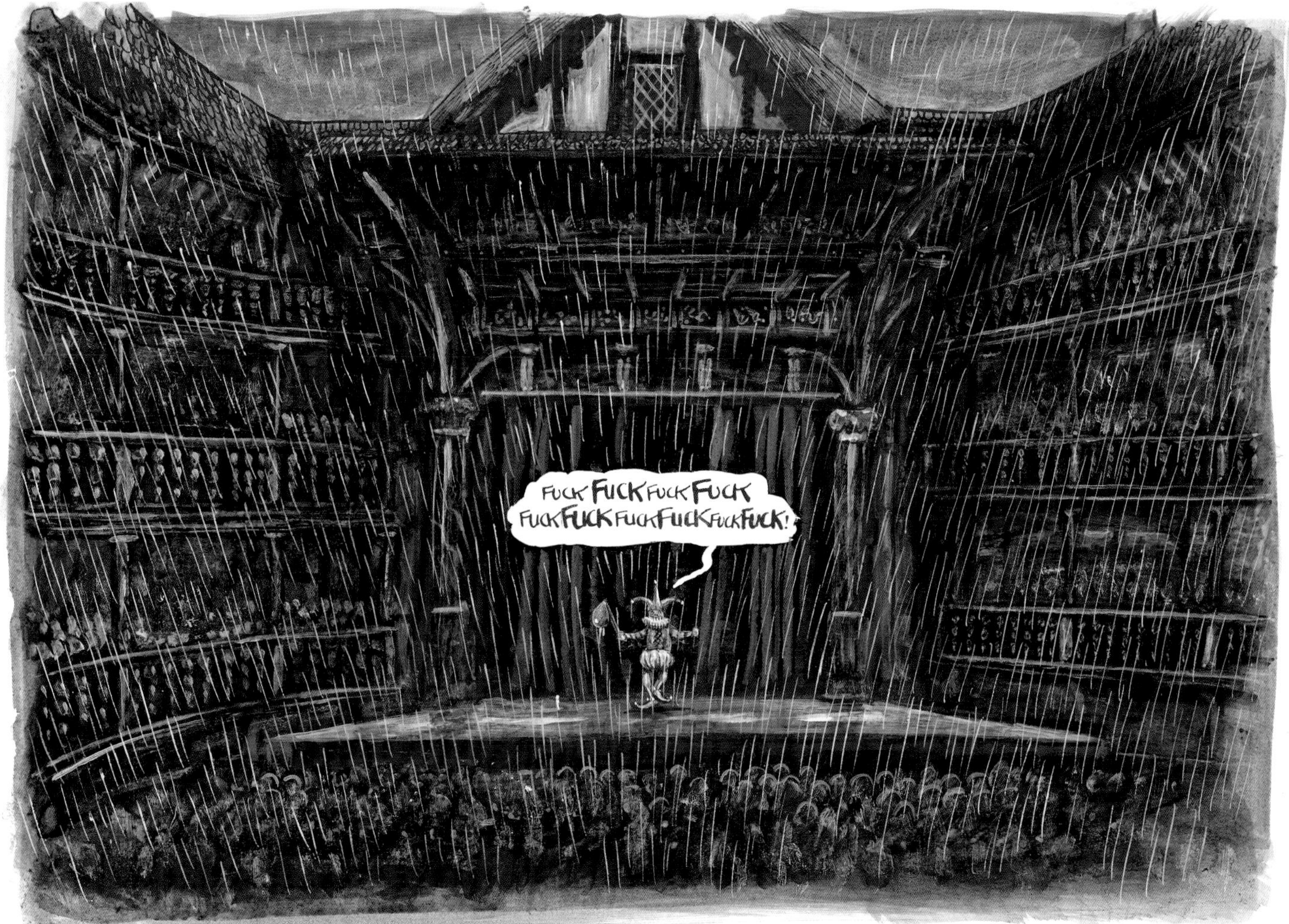
FUCK FUCK FUCK FUCK
FUCK FUCK FUCK FUCK FUCK FUCK!

The English Civil War

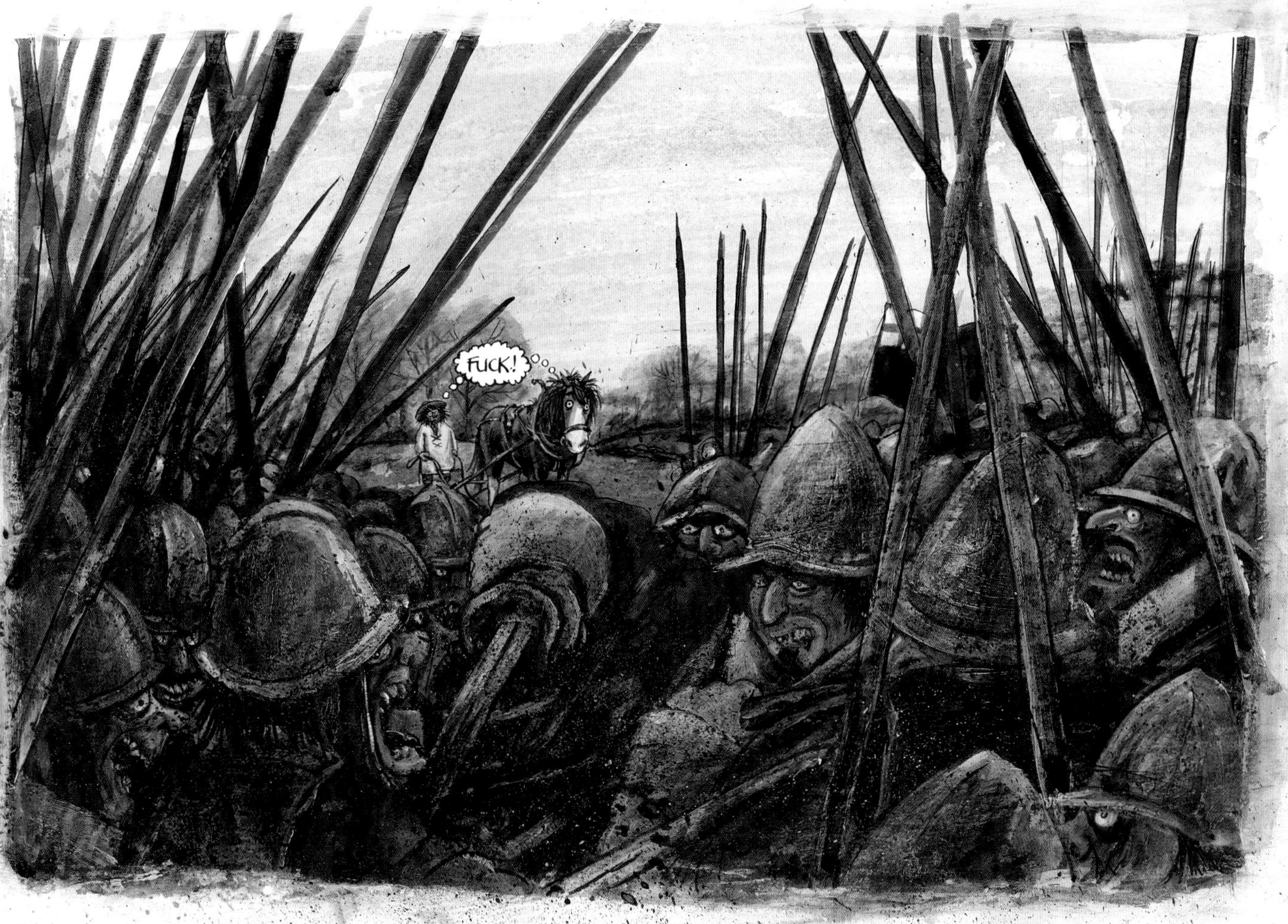
FUCK!

Newton Discovers the Law of Gravity

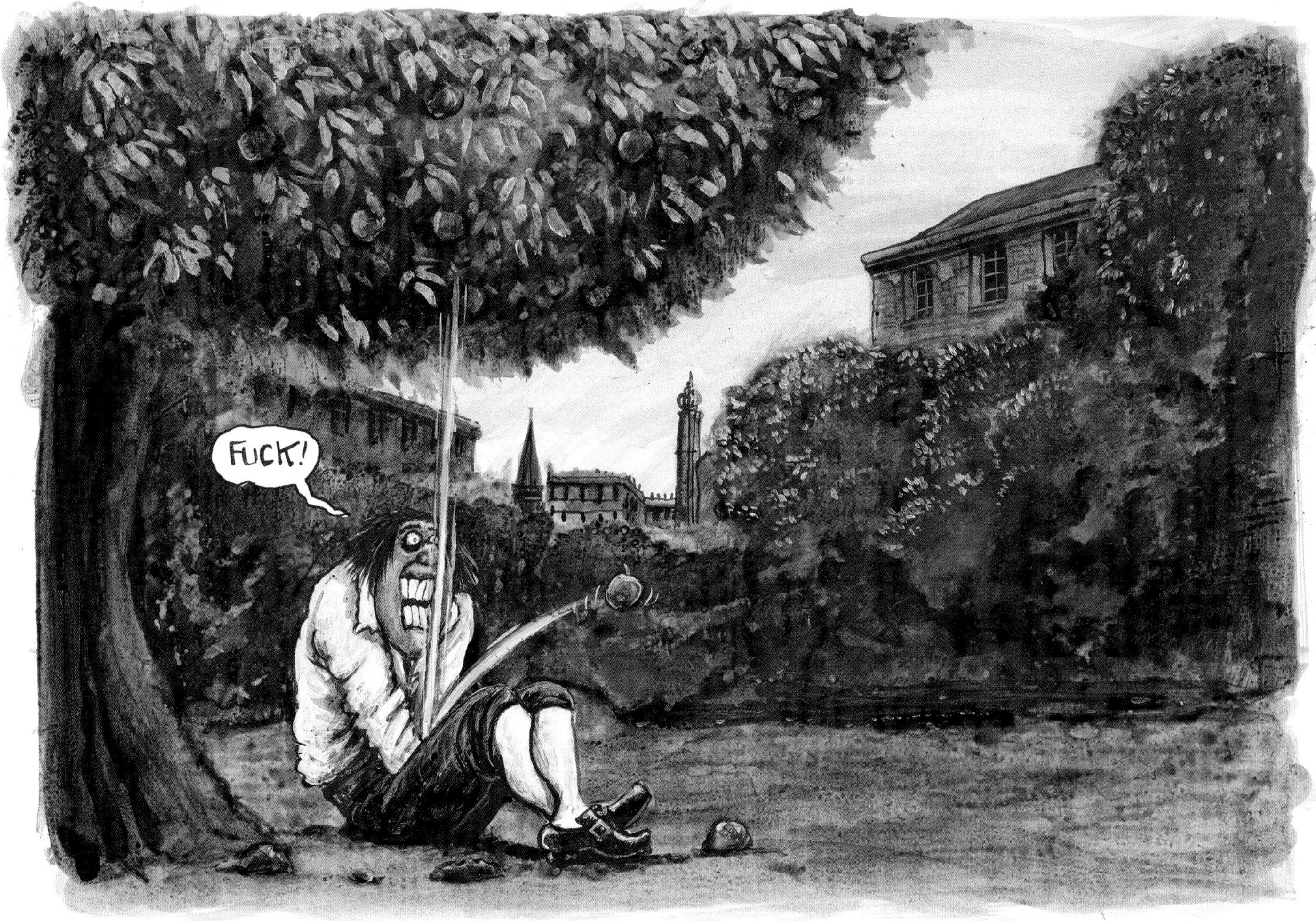
FUCK!

European Absolutism and the Court at Versailles

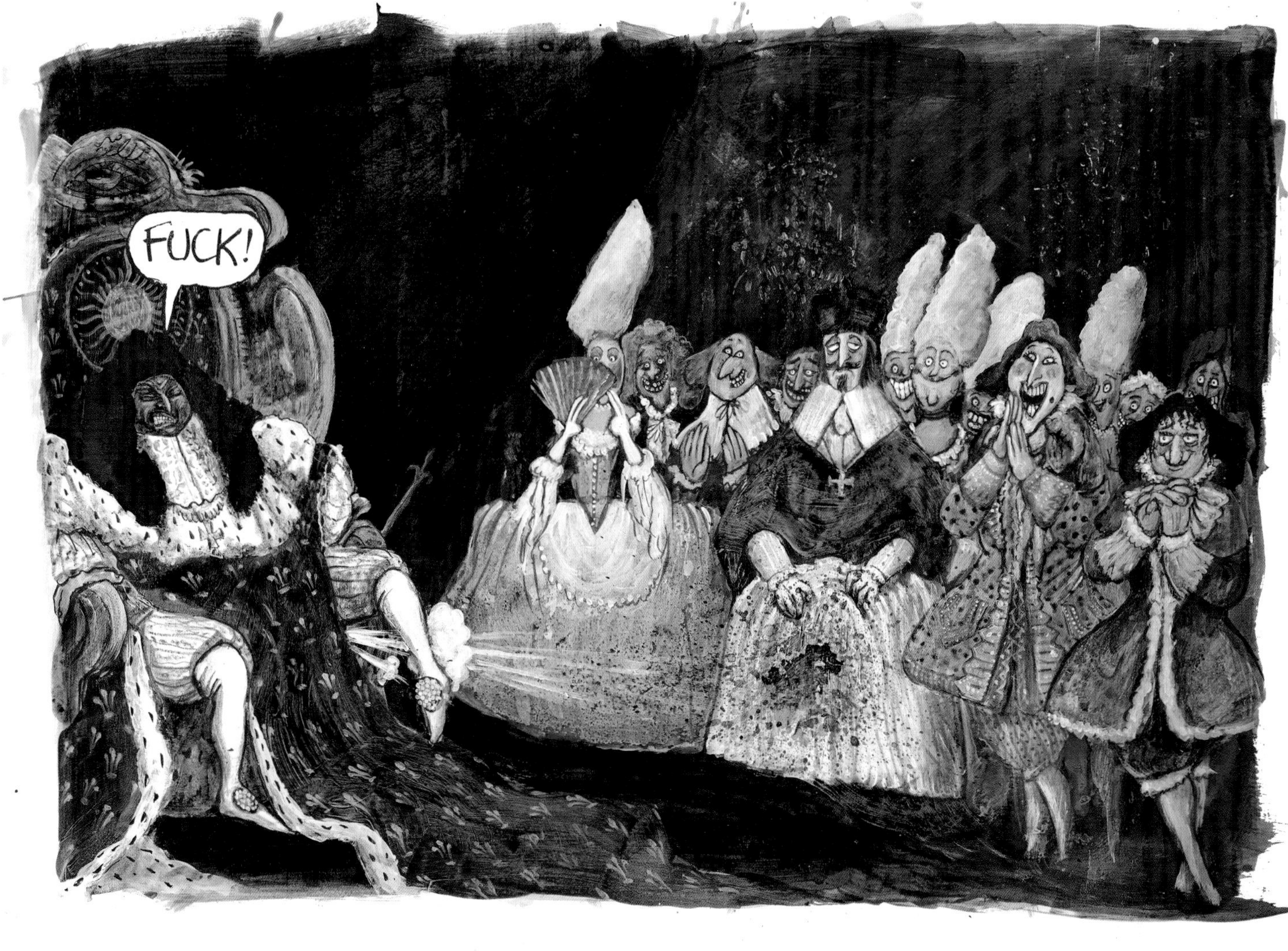
FUCK!

The Age of Reason

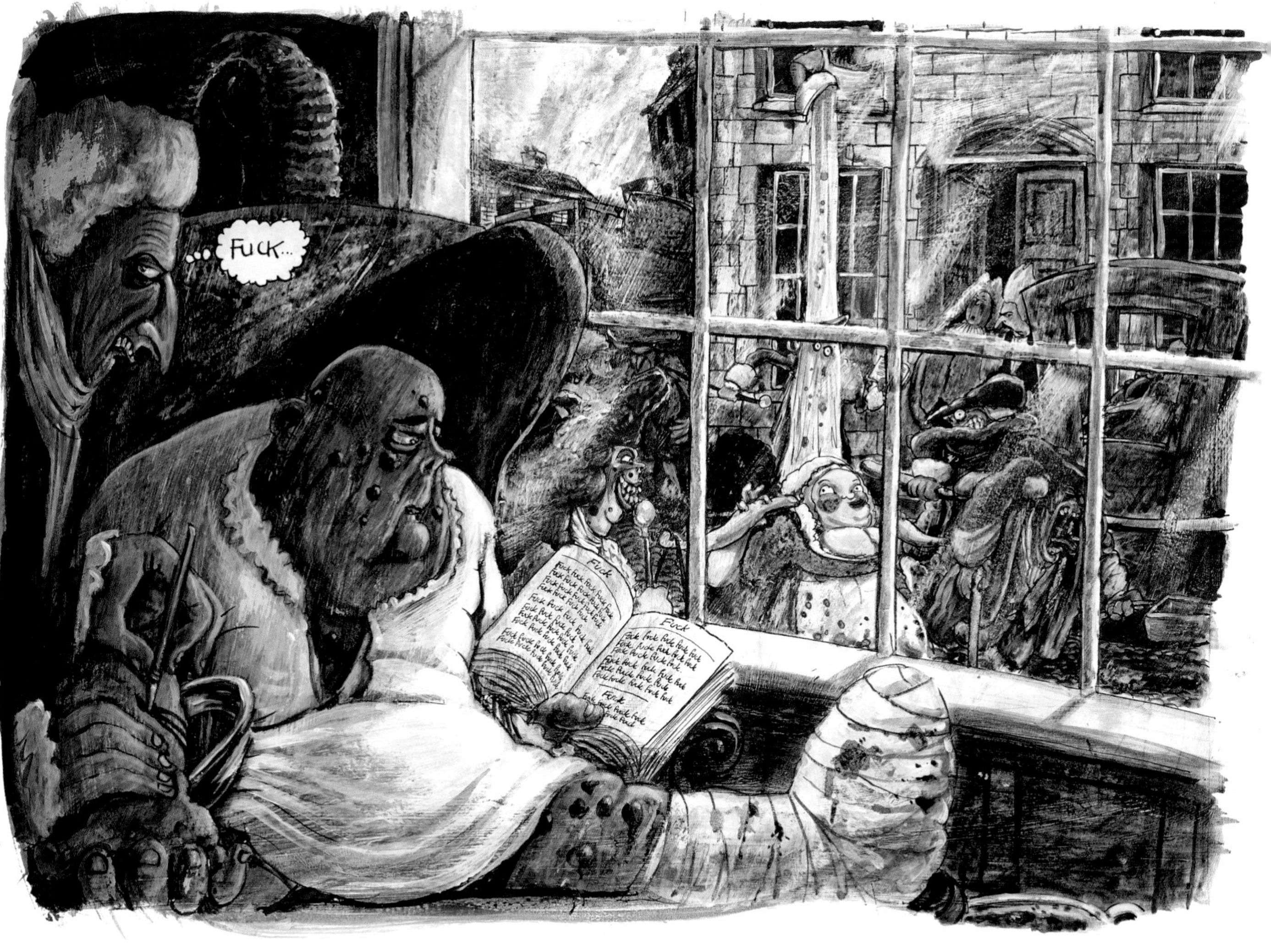

FUCK...
Fuck
Fuck
Fuck

The Expansion of European Trade

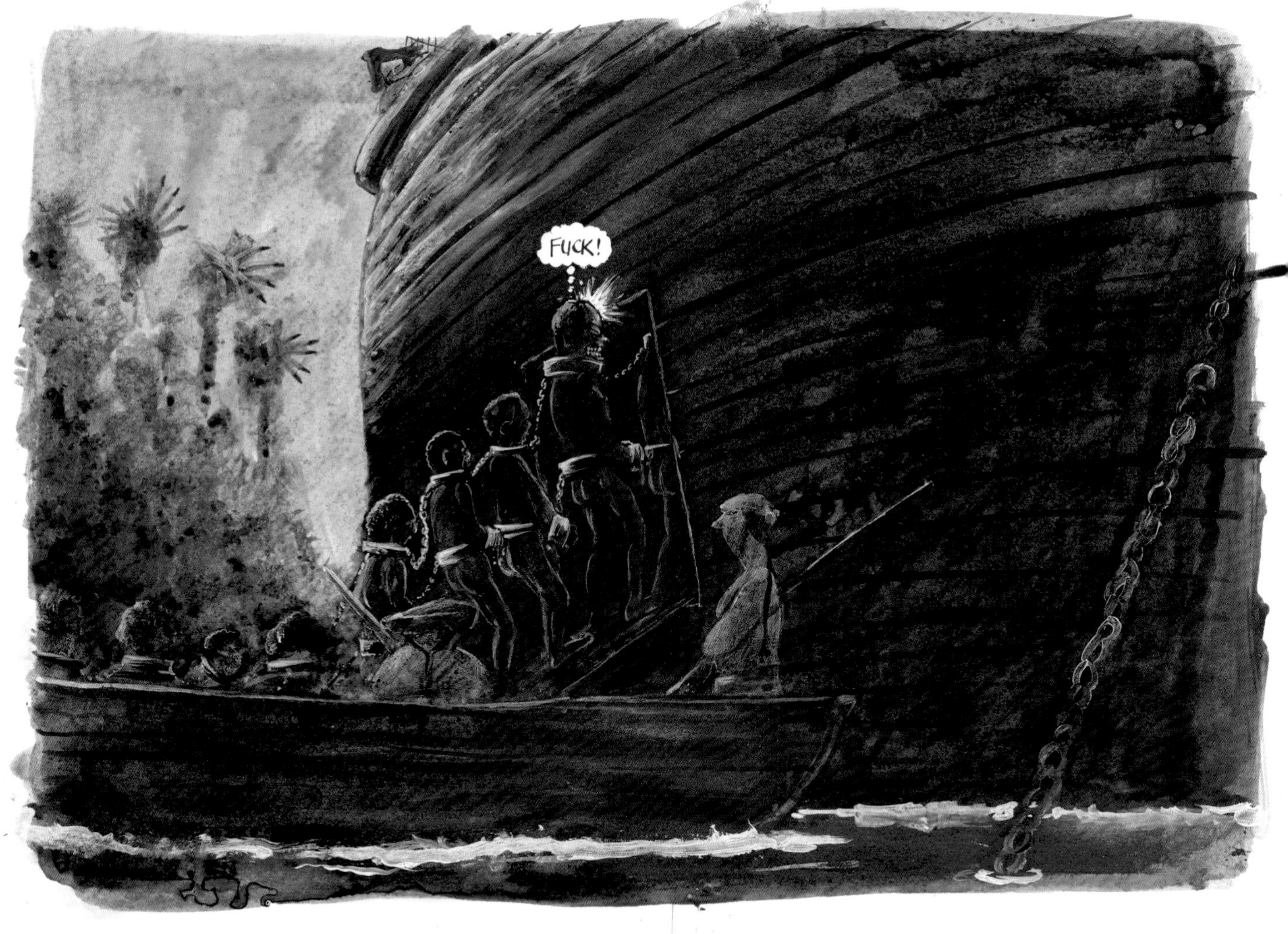
FUCK!

The French Revolution

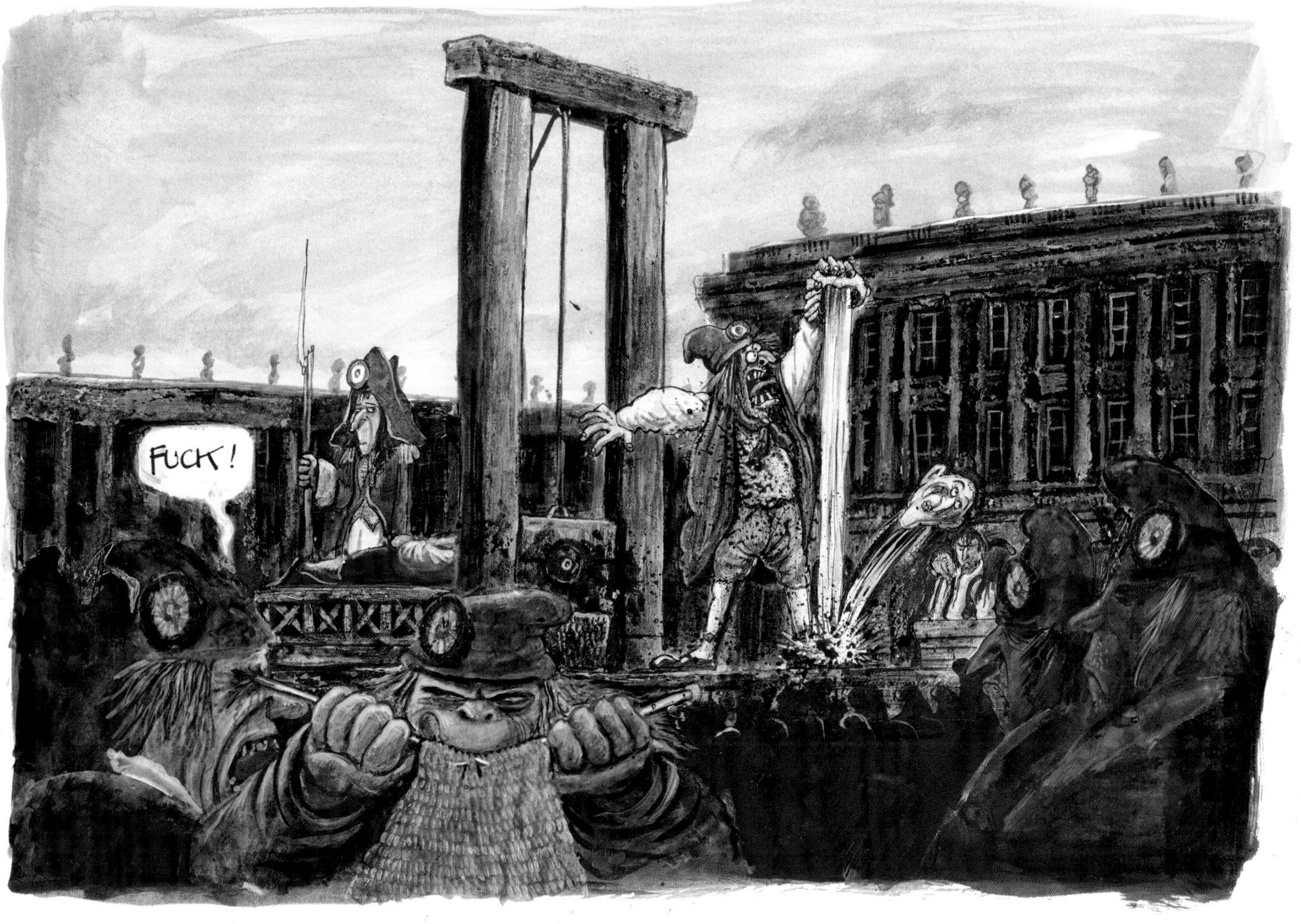
FUCK!

The Romantic Poets

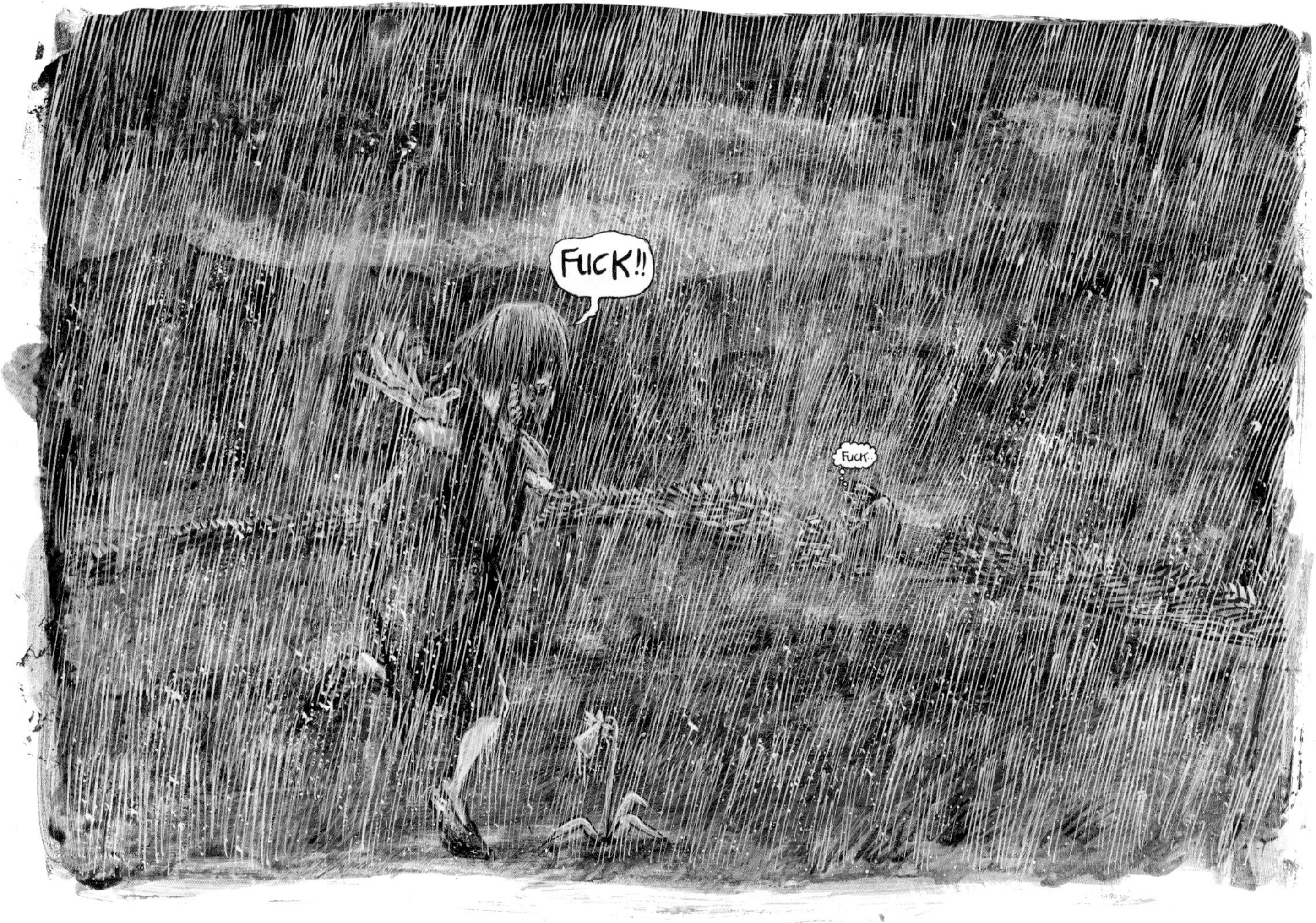
FUCK!!
FUCK.

The Napoleonic Wars

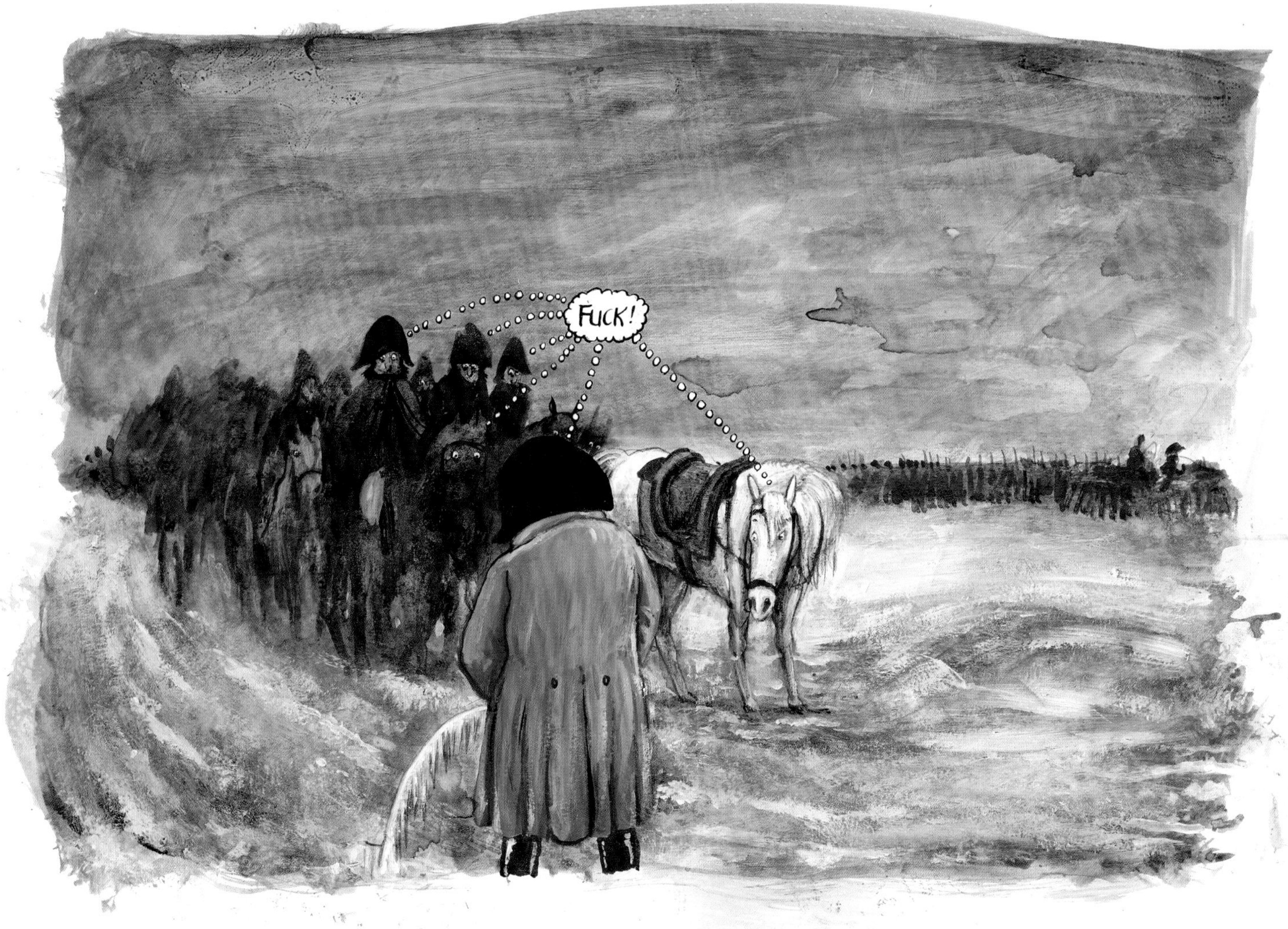
FUCK!

The Industrial Revolution

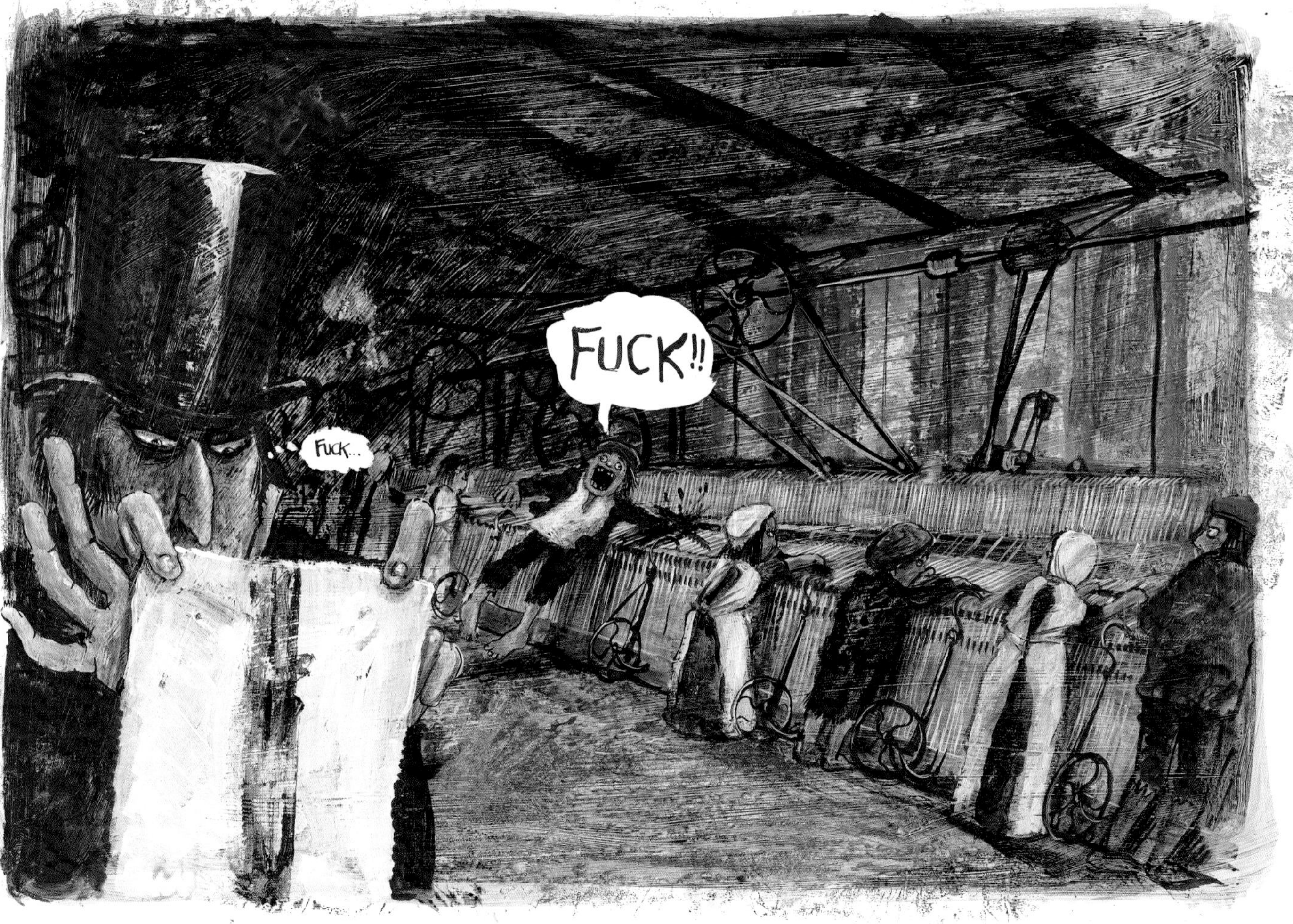
FUCK...
FUCK!!

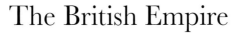

The British Empire

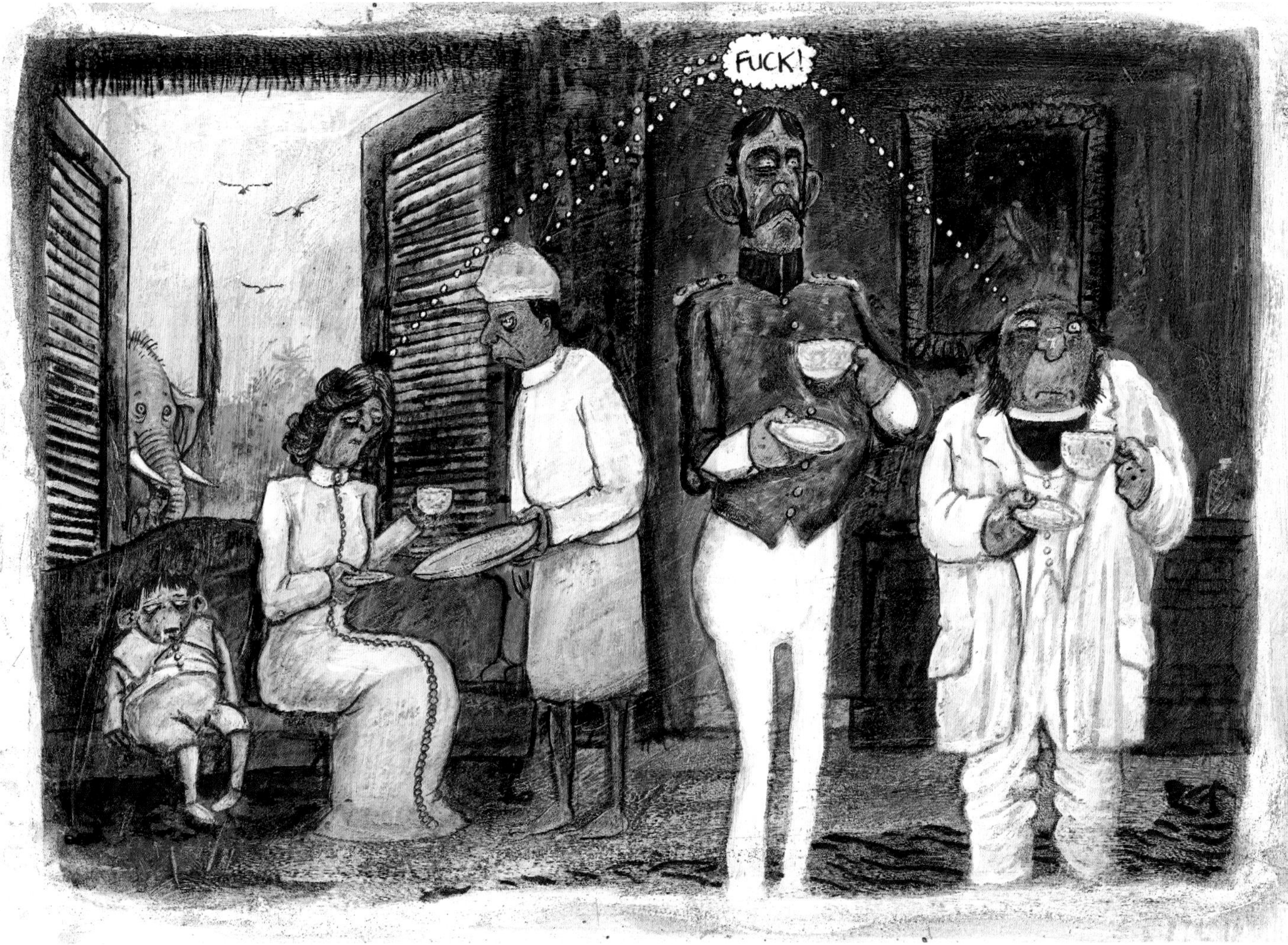
FUCK!

Alexander Graham Bell Invents the Telephone

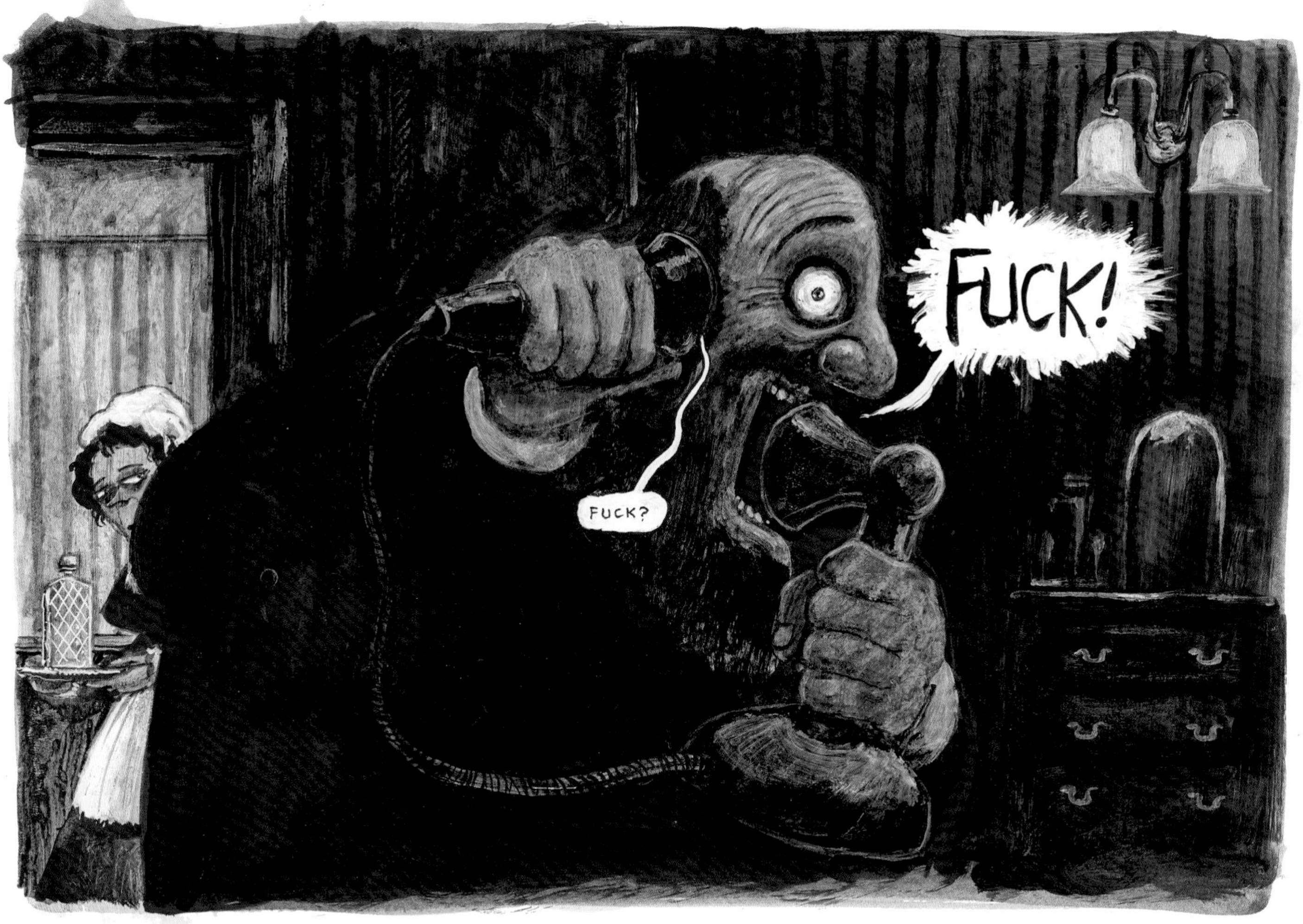
FUCK!
FUCK?

The Impressionists

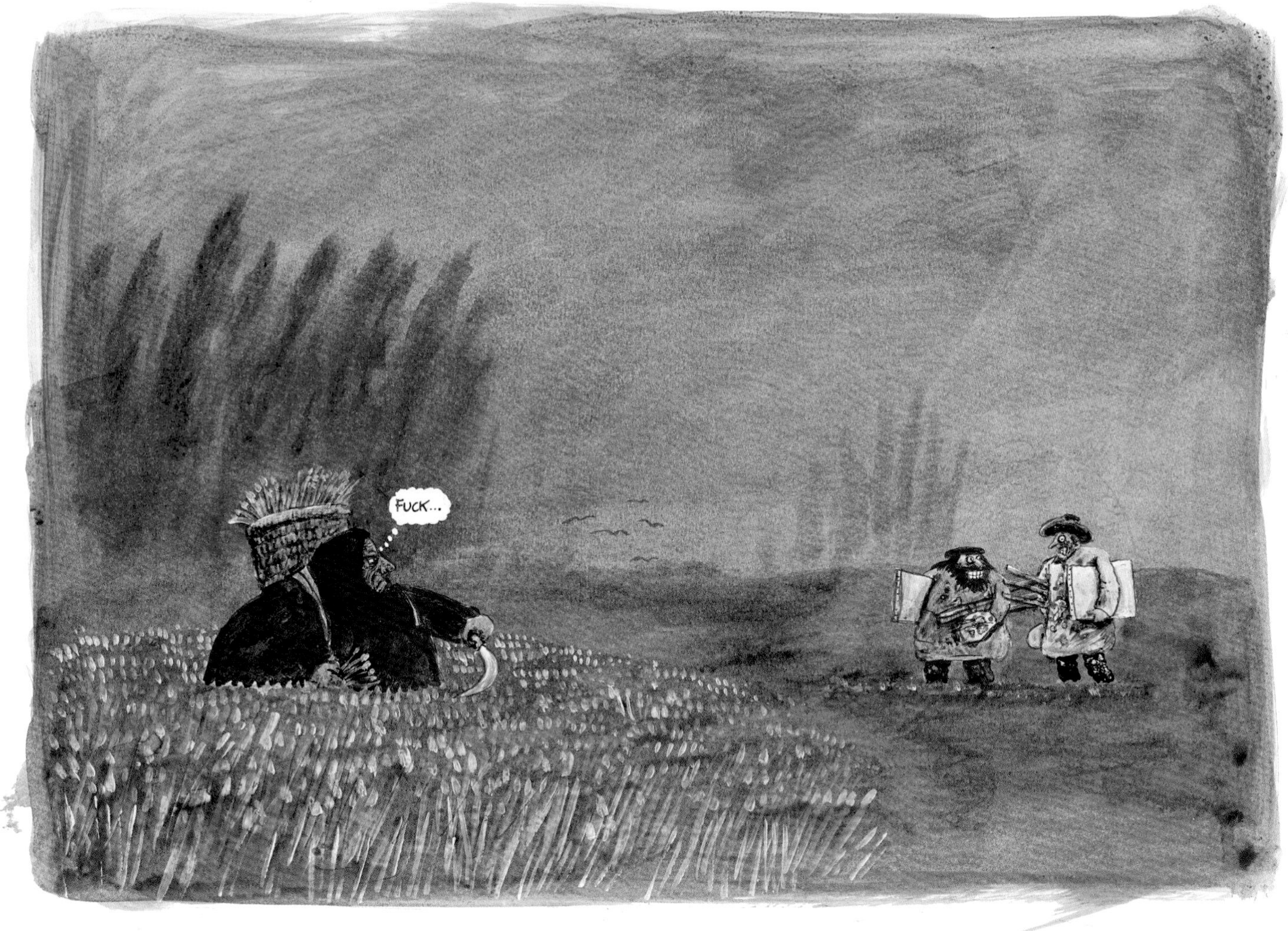
FUCK...

London: The Capital of Empire

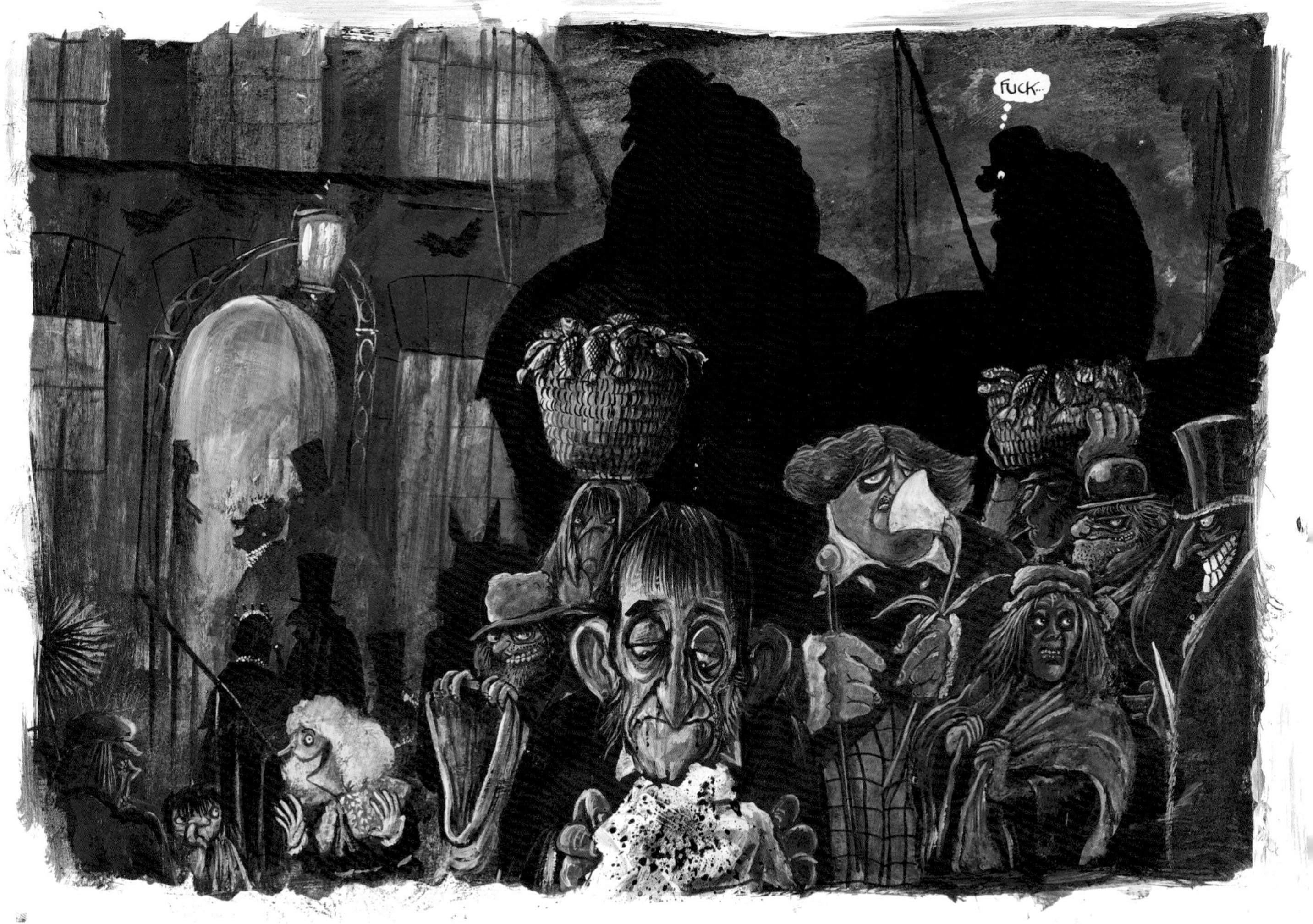
FUCK...

Freud Unlocks the Secrets of the Mind

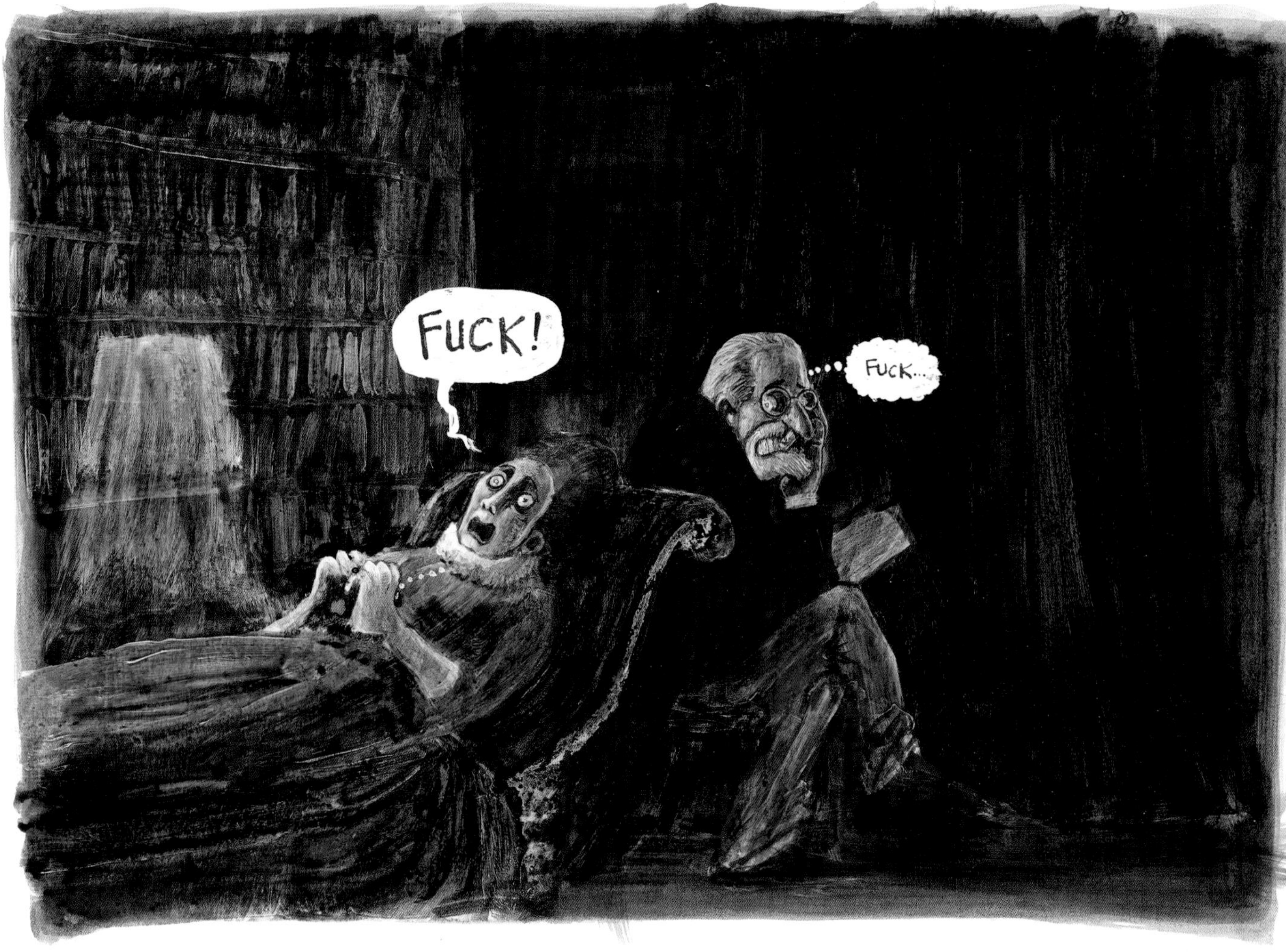
FUCK!
FUCK...

The Wright Brothers Conquer the Air

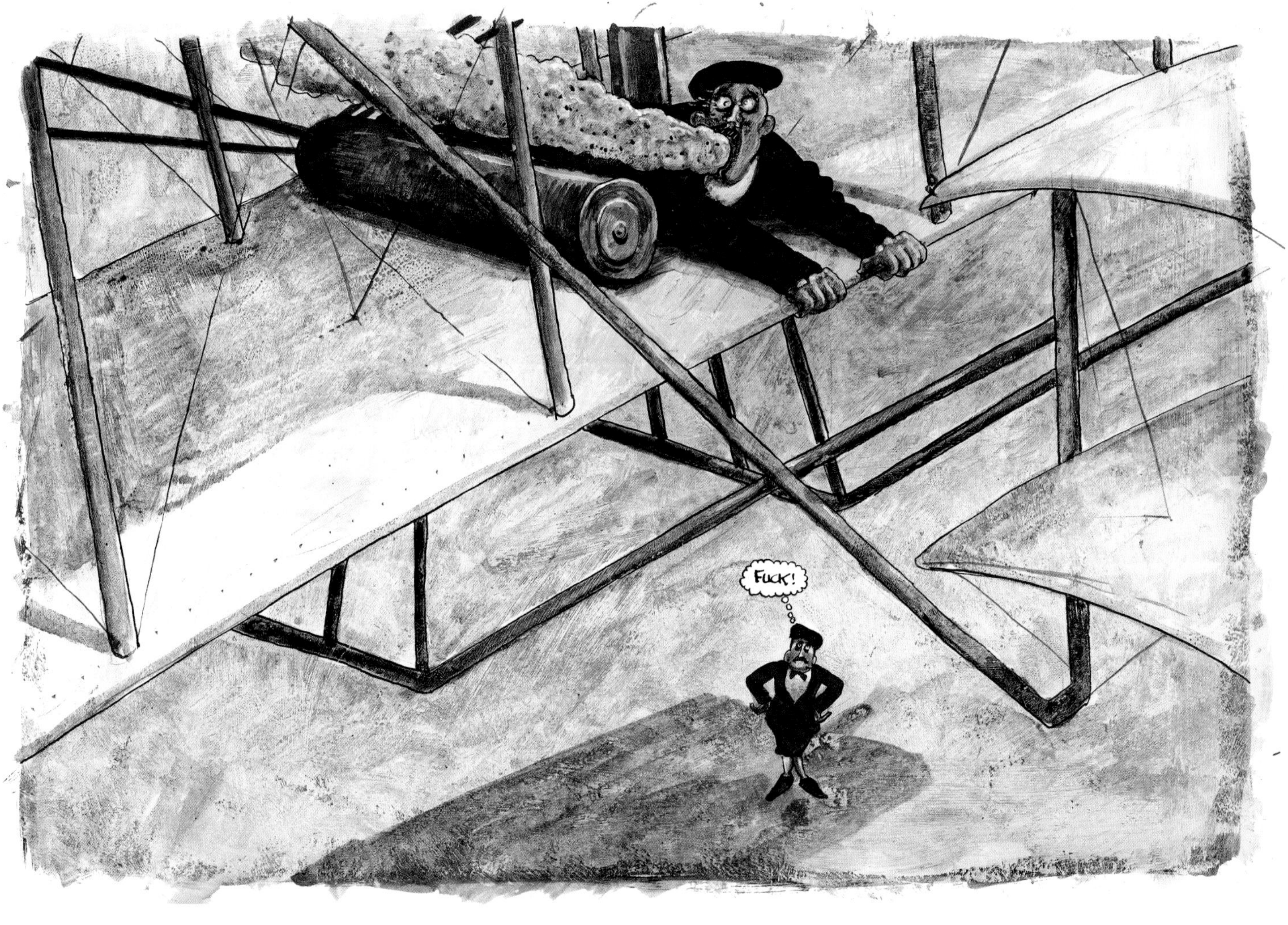
FUCK!

Oates Leaves Captain Scott's Tent

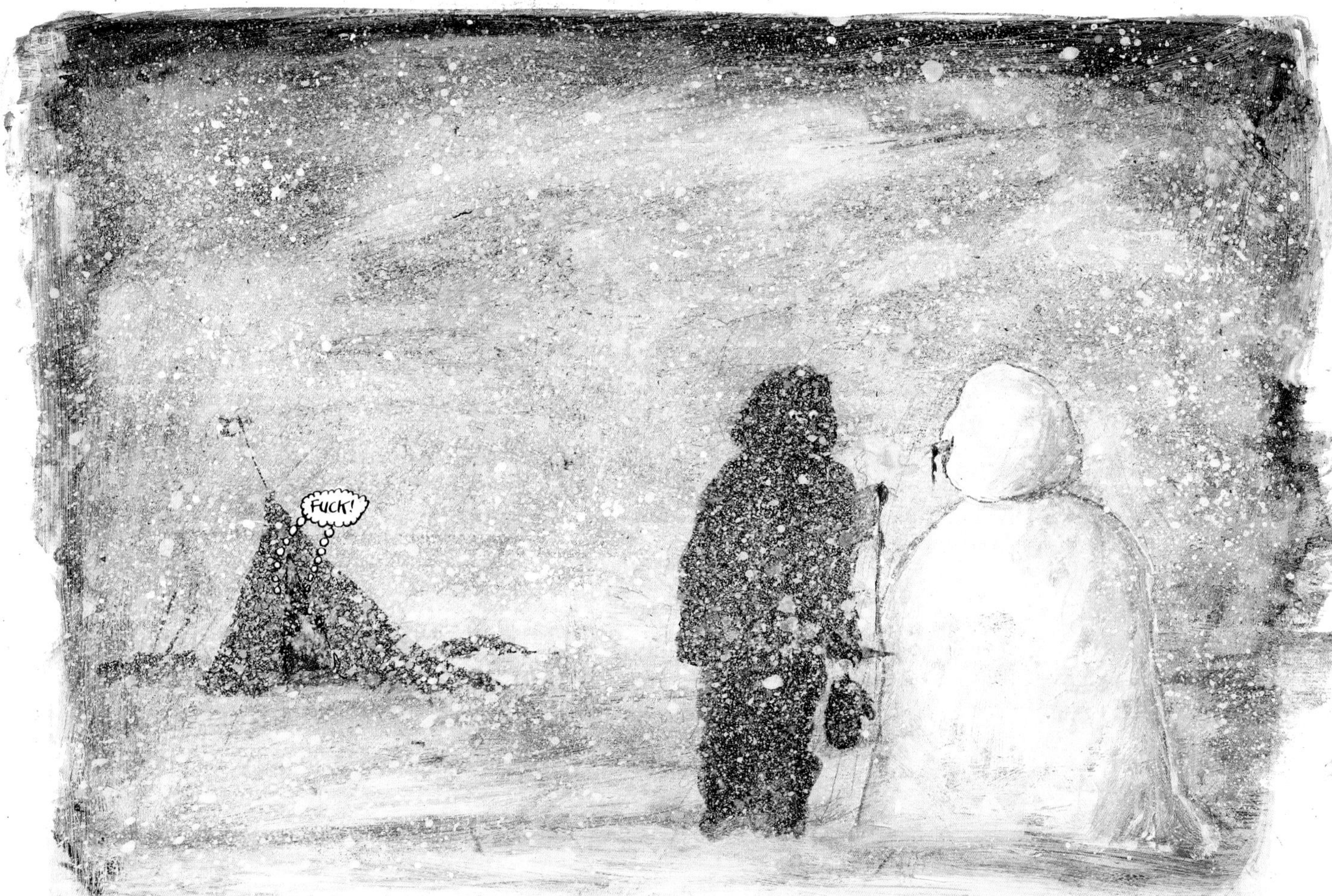
FUCK!

The Great War

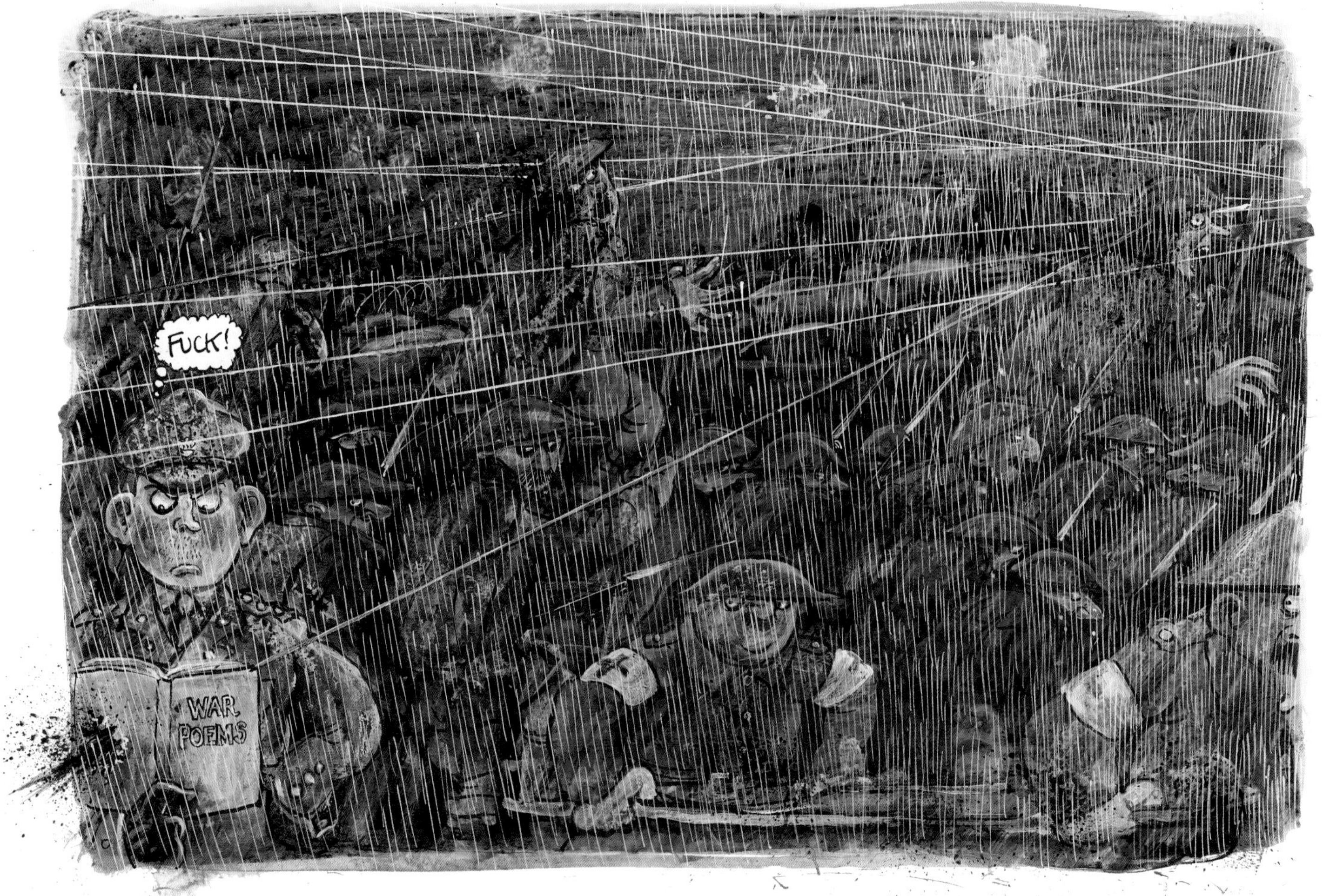
FUCK!
WAR POEMS

The Great Depression

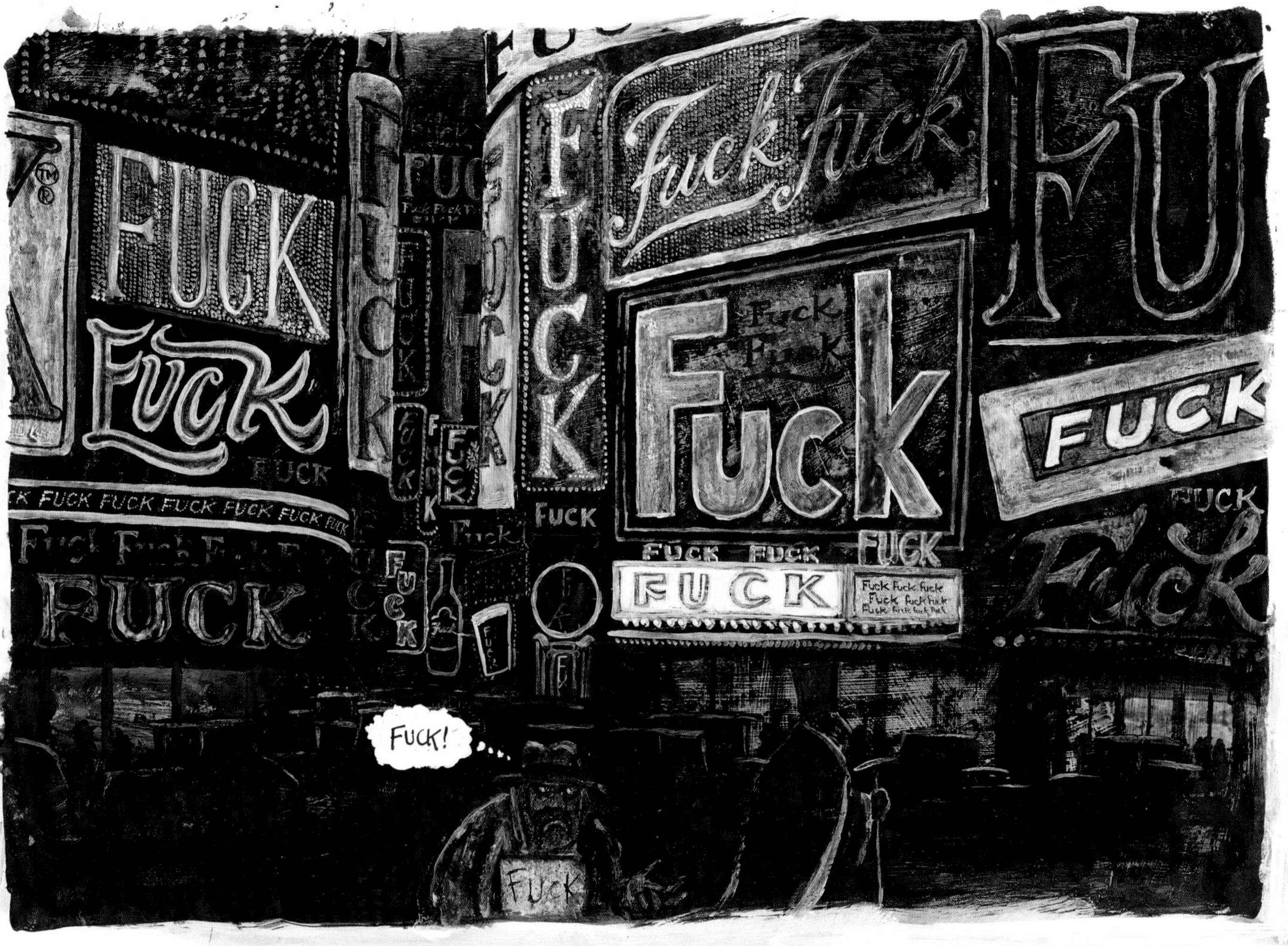
FUCK
Fuck
FUCK
FUCK FUCK FUCK FUCK FUCK
FUCK
FUCK
FUCK
FUCK
FUCK
Fuck Fuck
Fuck
FUCK
Fuck
FUCK
FUCK FUCK FUCK
FUCK
Fuck fuck fuck
Fuck fuck fuck
FU
FUCK
FUCK
Fuck
FUCK!
FUCK

Man's Inhumanity to Man

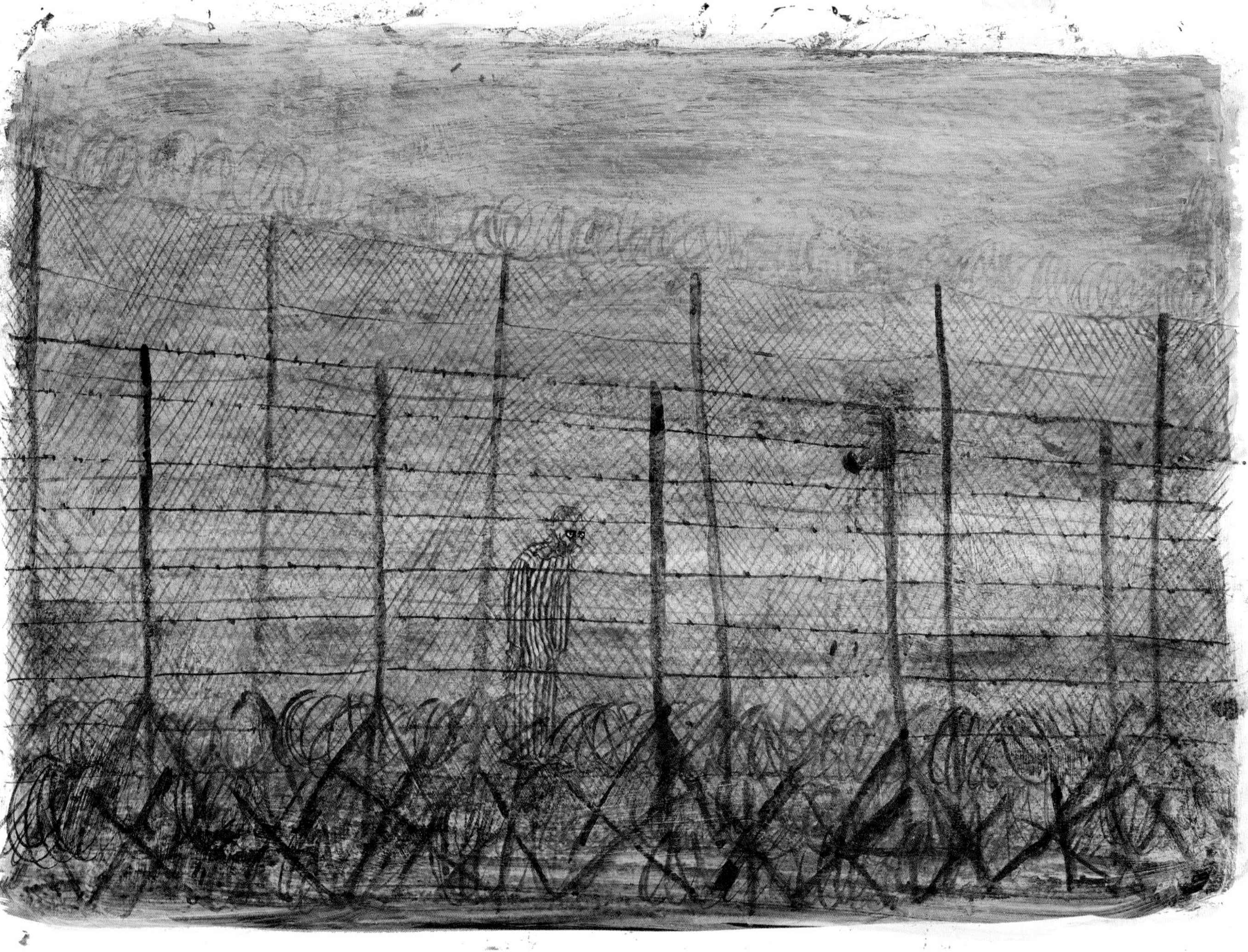

Man Harnesses the Power of the Atom

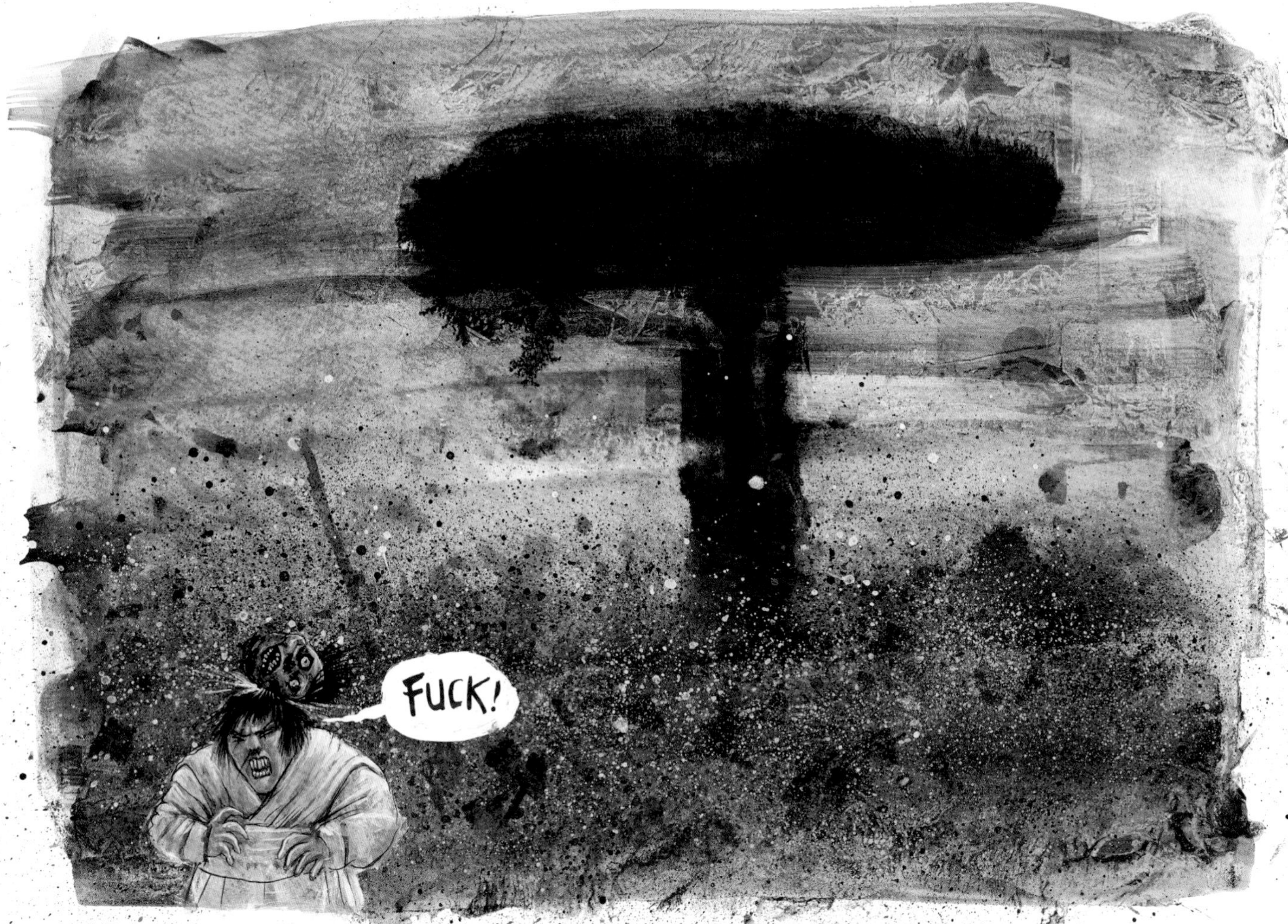
FUCK!

The Great Society

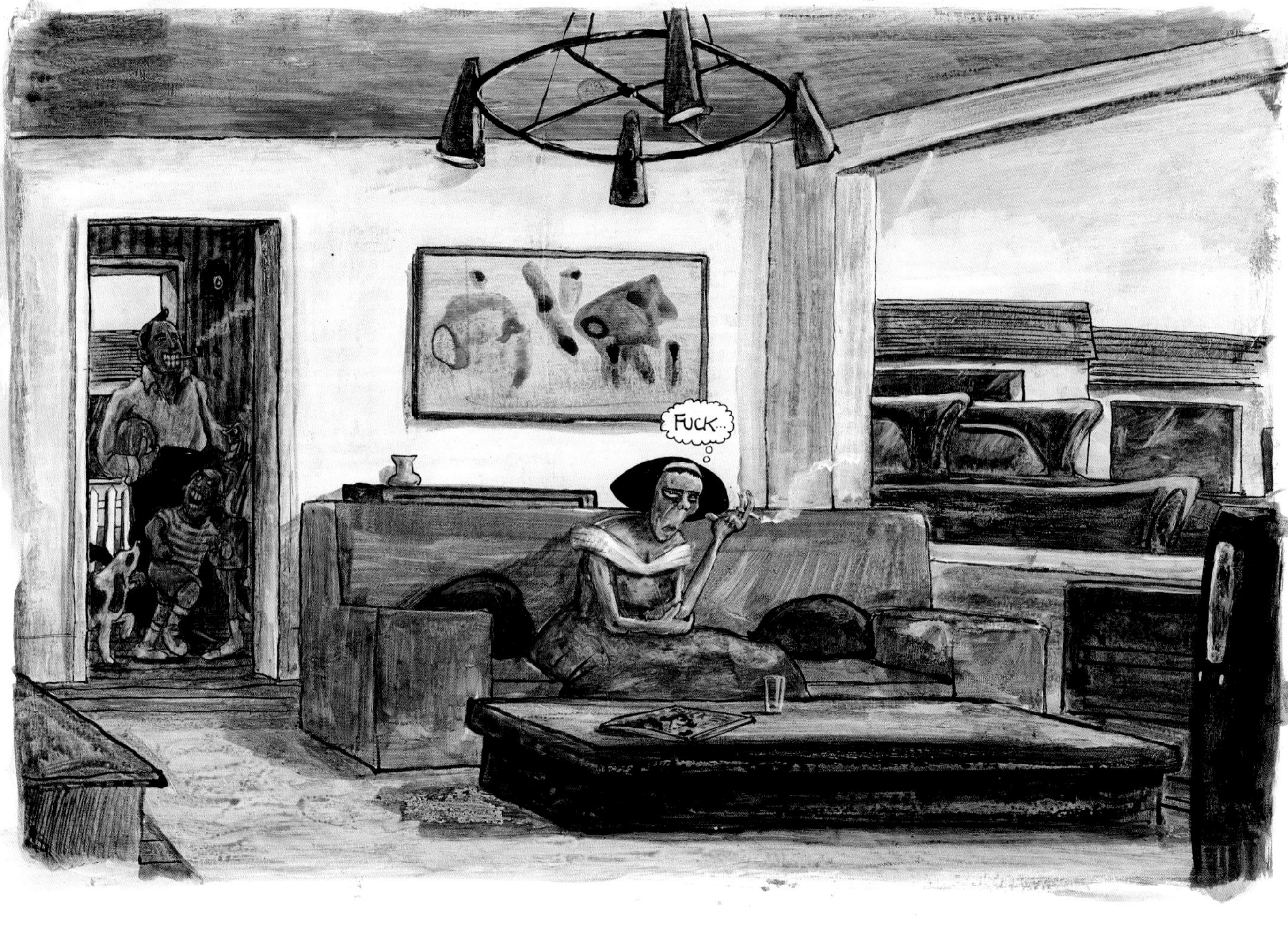
FUCK...

The Consumer Revolution

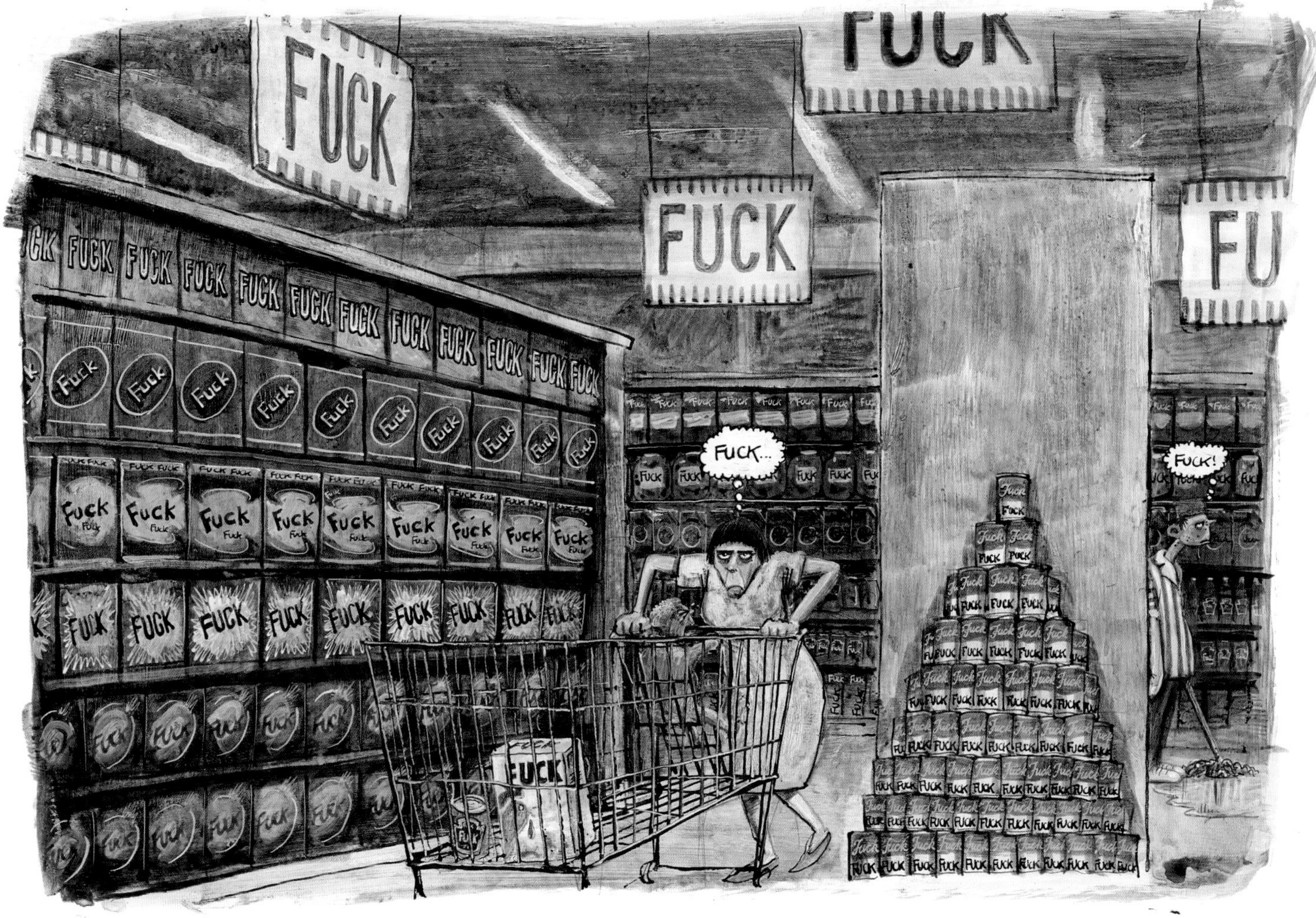
FUCK
FUCK
FUCK...
FUCK!
FUCK

The Conquest of Space

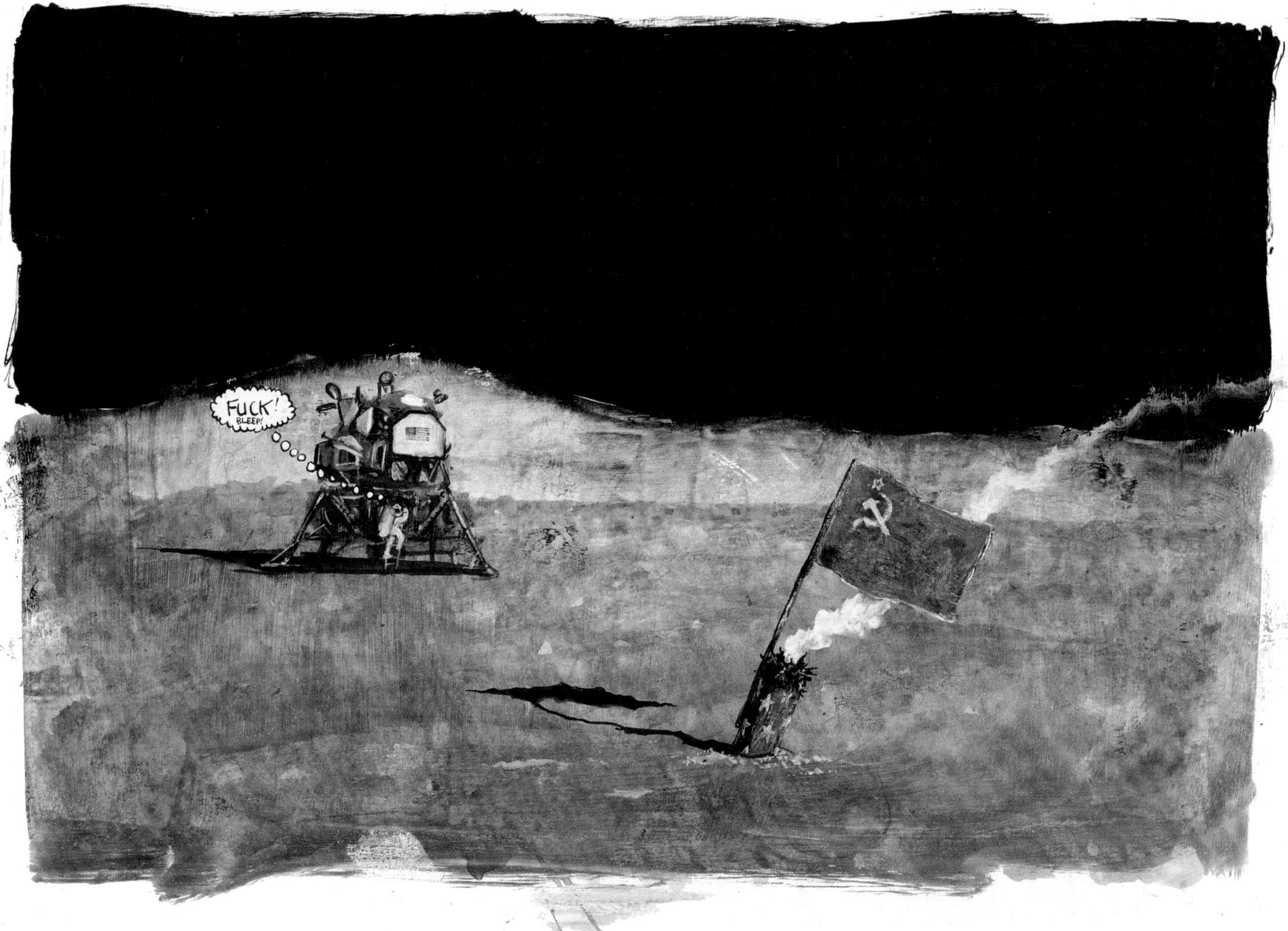

FUCK!
BLEEP!

Democracy in Action

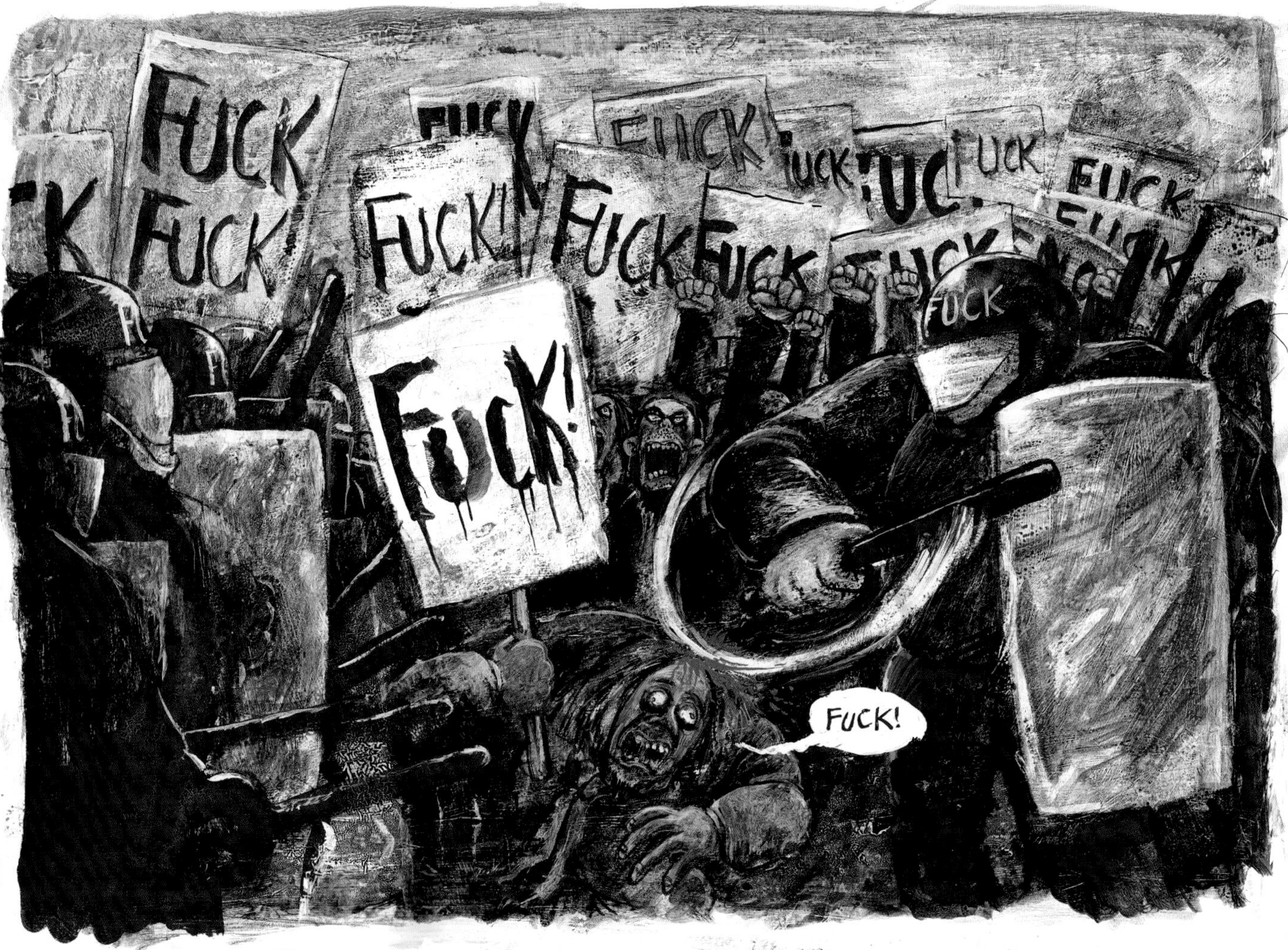
FUCK
FUCK
FUCK!
FUCK
FUCK
FUCK!
FUCK
FUCK!

Live Aid

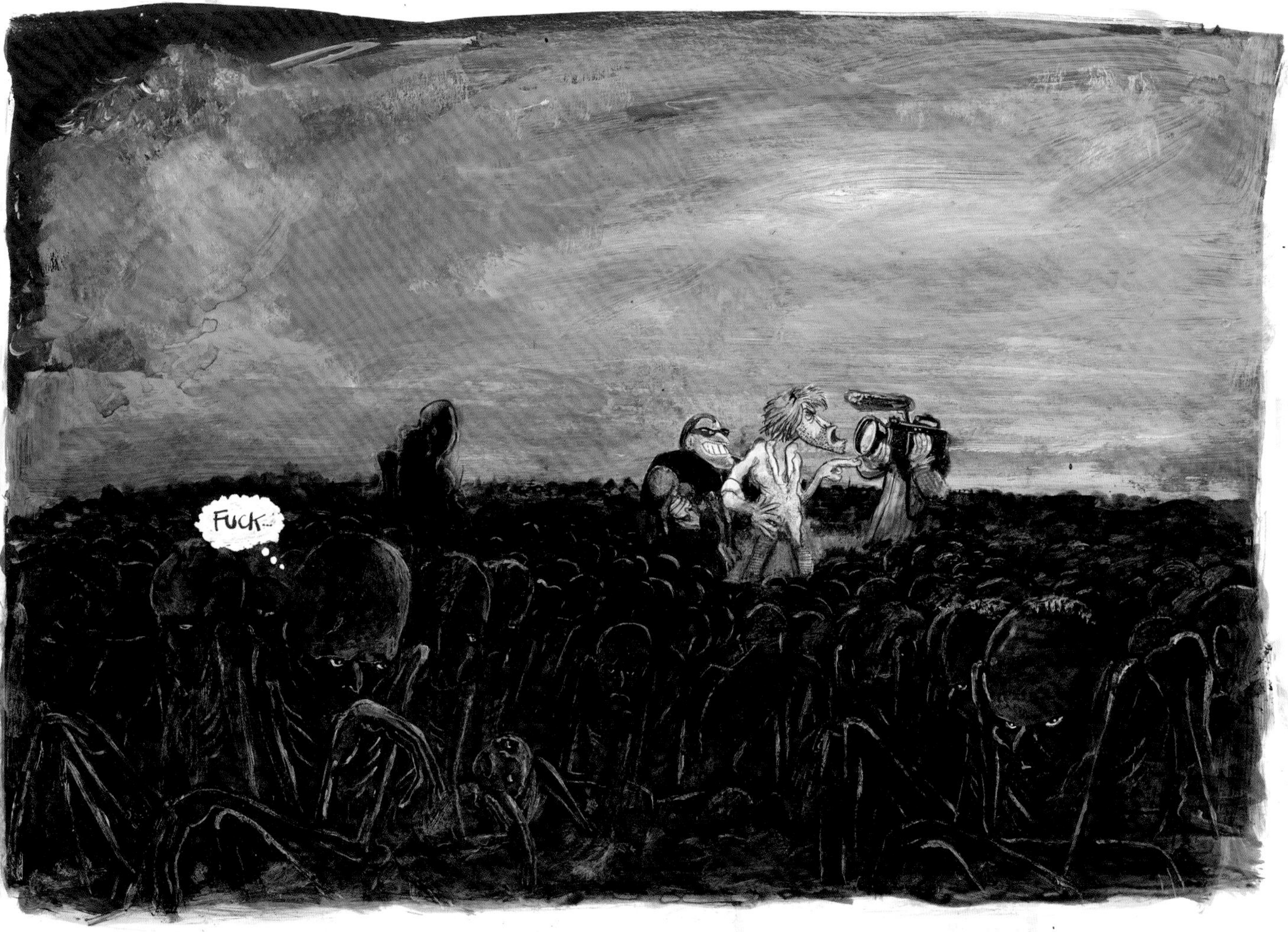
FUCK...

The Developing World

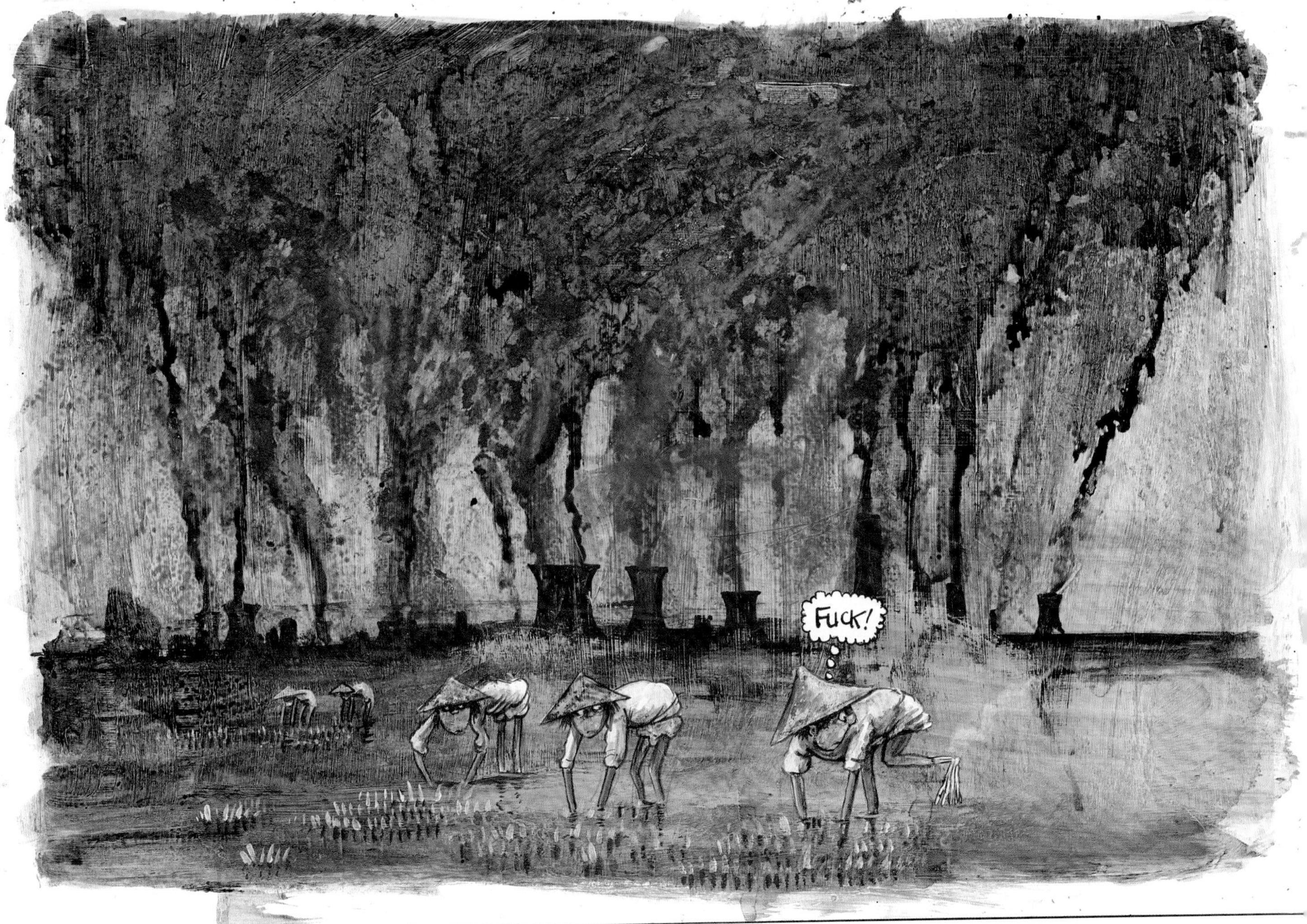
FUCK!

Humanitarian Interventionism

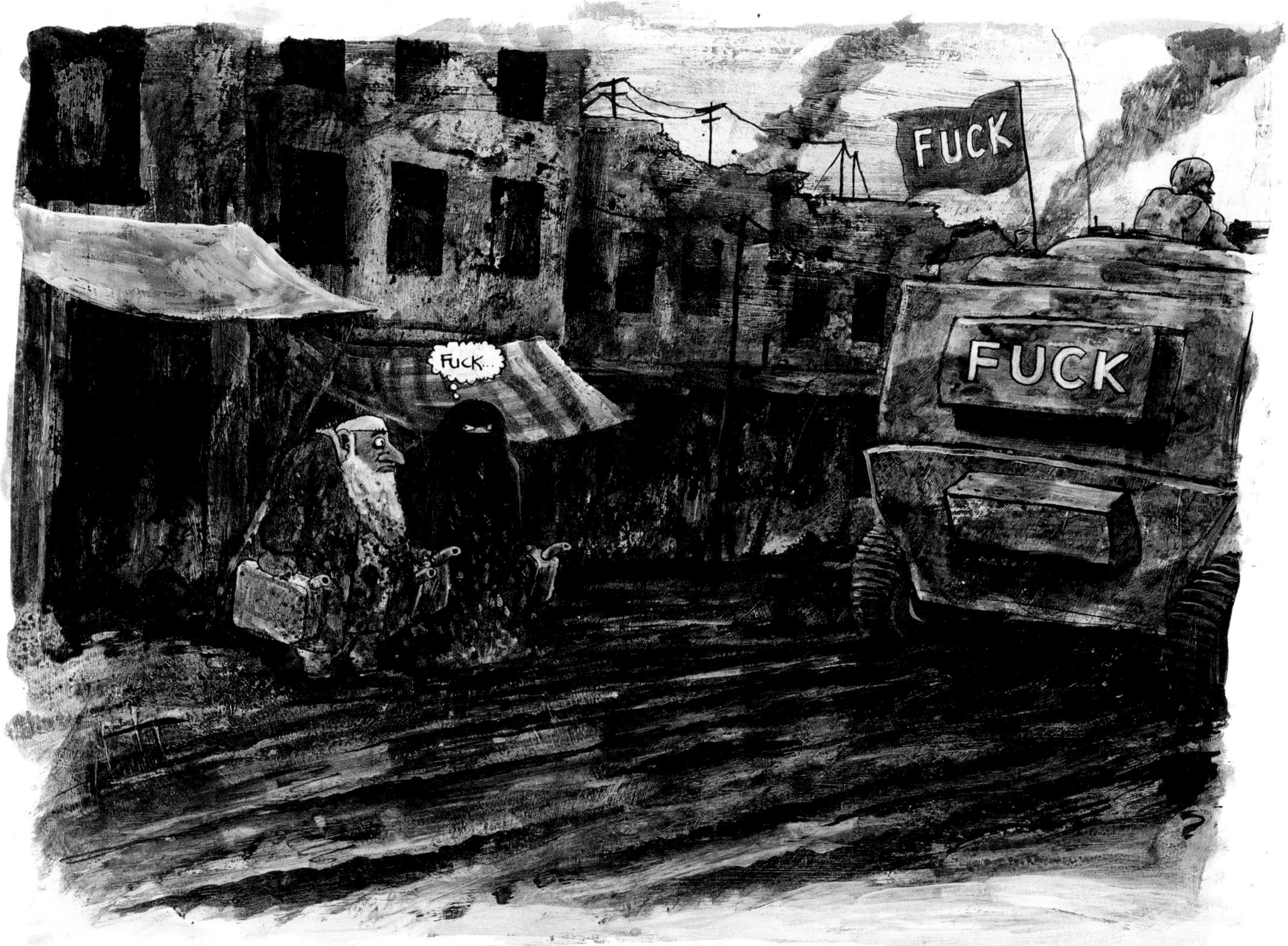
FUCK
FUCK...
FUCK

The War on Terror

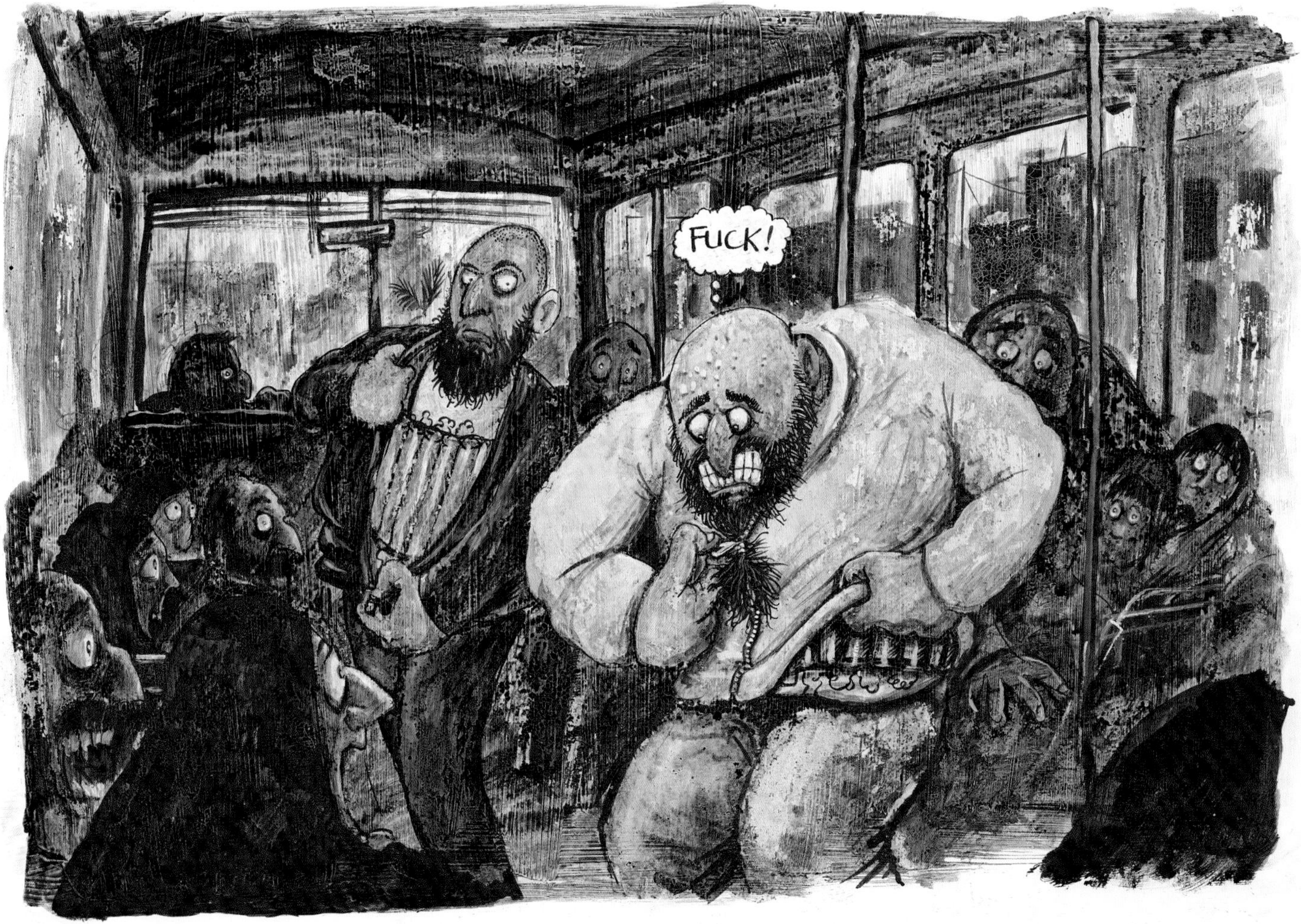
FUCK!

The Information Revolution

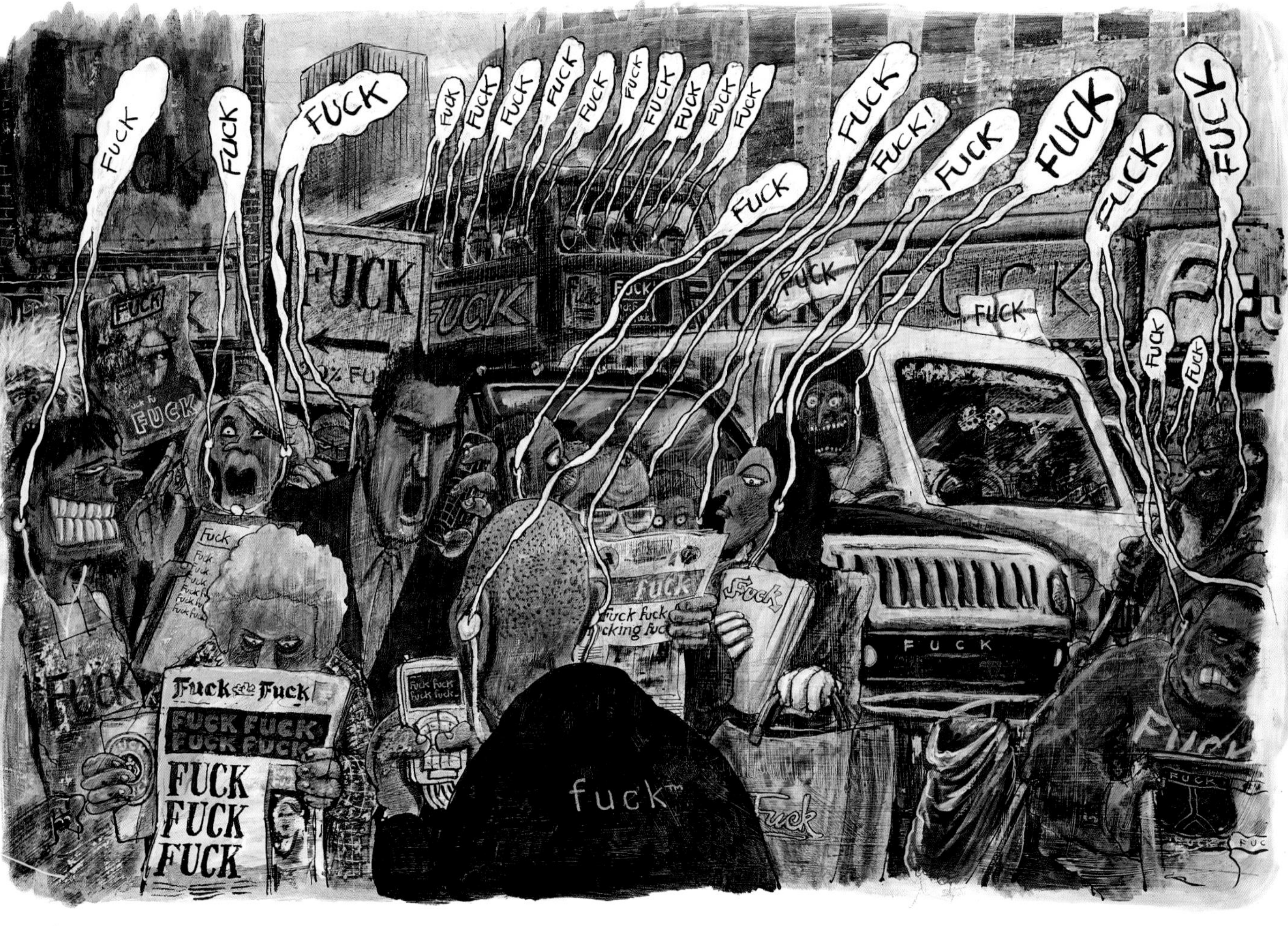
FUCK
FUCK
FUCK
FUCK
FUCK
FUCK
FUCK
FUCK
FUCK
FUCK
FUCK
FUCK
FUCK
FUCK
FUCK!
FUCK
FUCK
FUCK
FUCK
FUCK
FUCK
FUCK
FUCK
FUCK
FUCK
FUCK
Fuck
Fuck
FUCK FUCK
FUCK FUCK
FUCK
FUCK
FUCK
Fuck fuck
fuck fuck
FUCK
Fuck fuck
Fuck
FUCK
fuck™
FUCK

Globalization

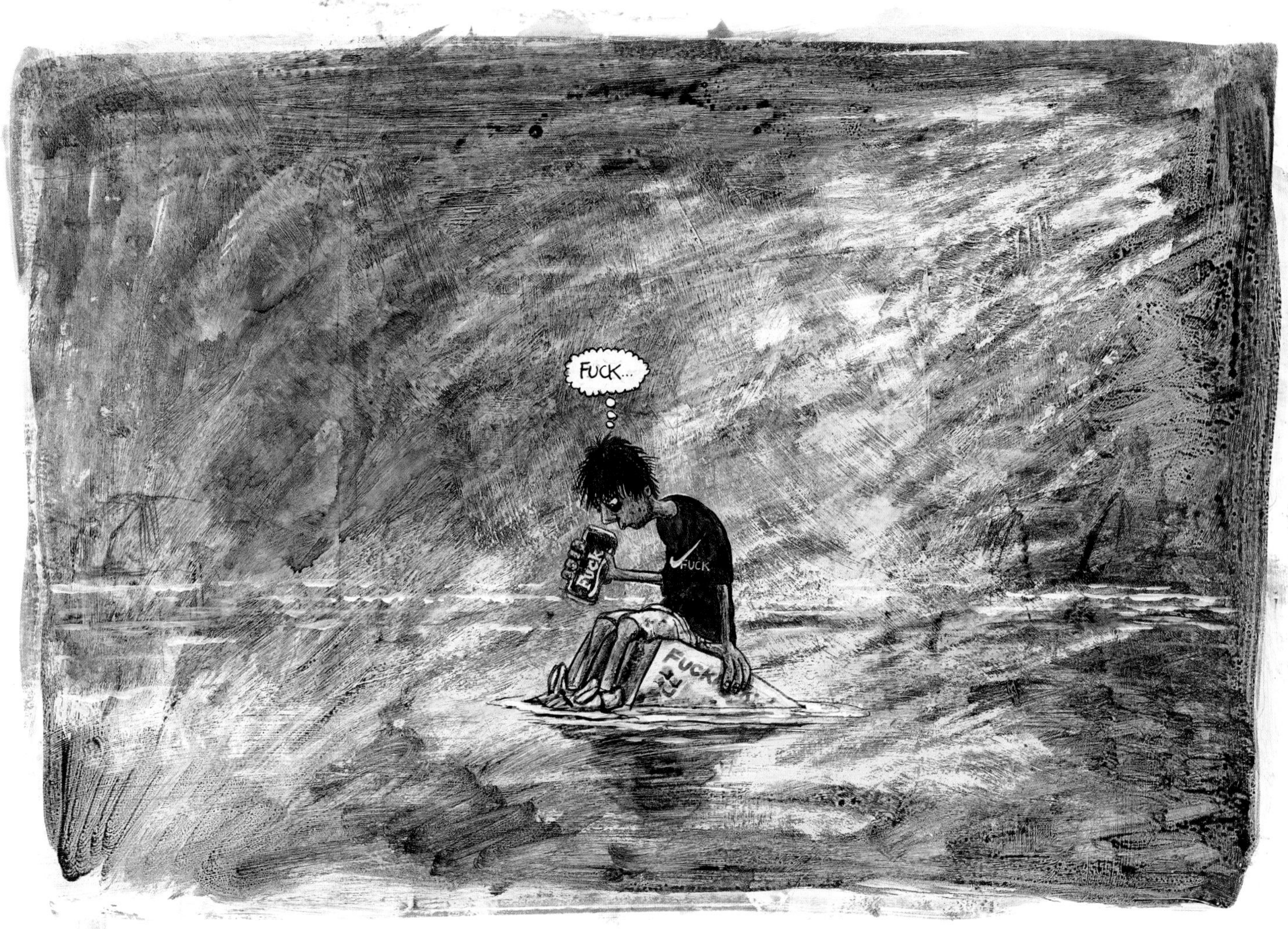
FUCK...
FUCK
FUCK
FUCK

Man Harnesses the Power of Genetics

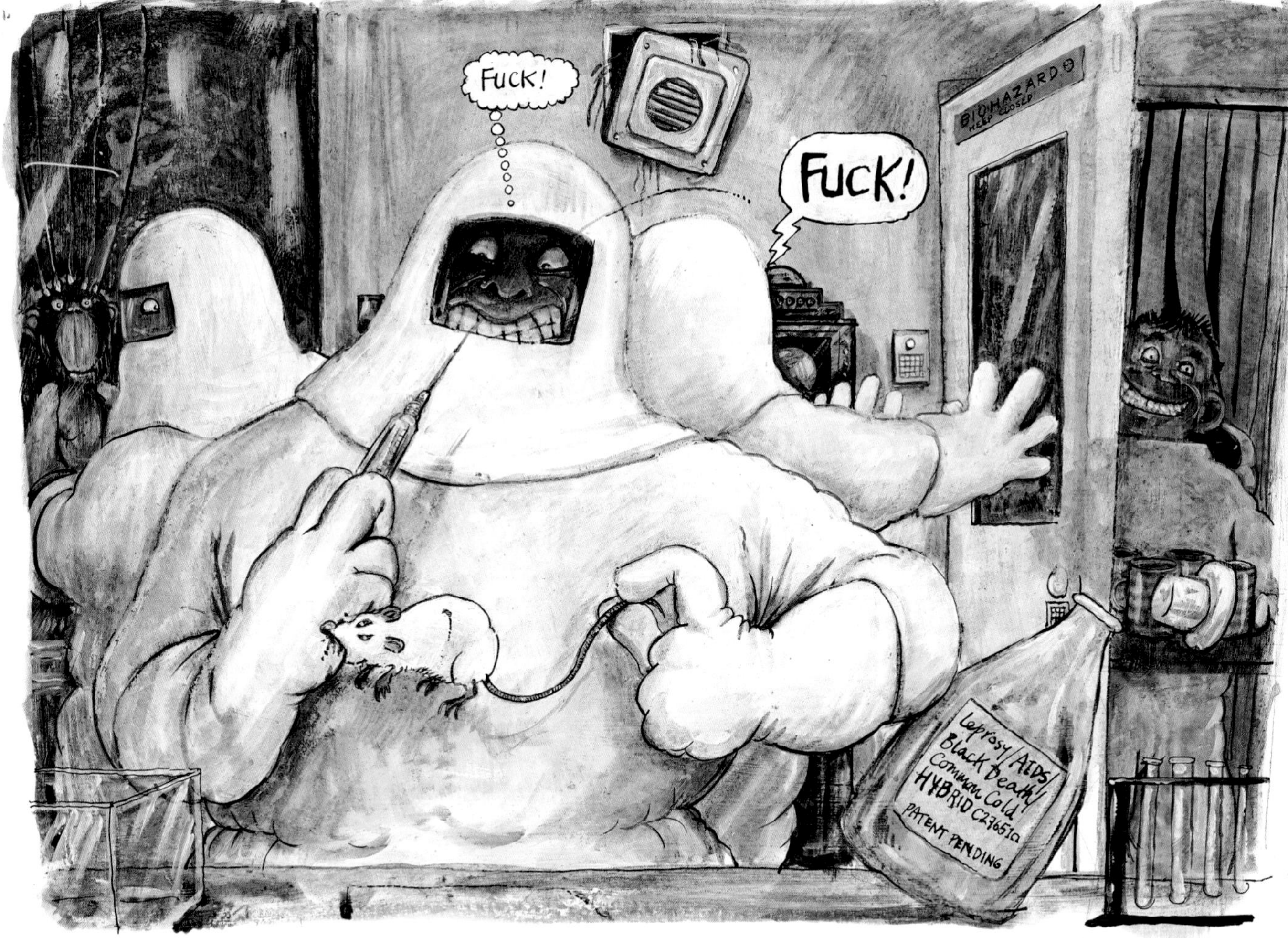
FUCK!
FUCK!
BIOHAZARD
KEEP CLOSED
Leprosy/AIDS/
Black Death/
Common Cold
HYBRID C27651a
PATENT PENDING

A New Ecology

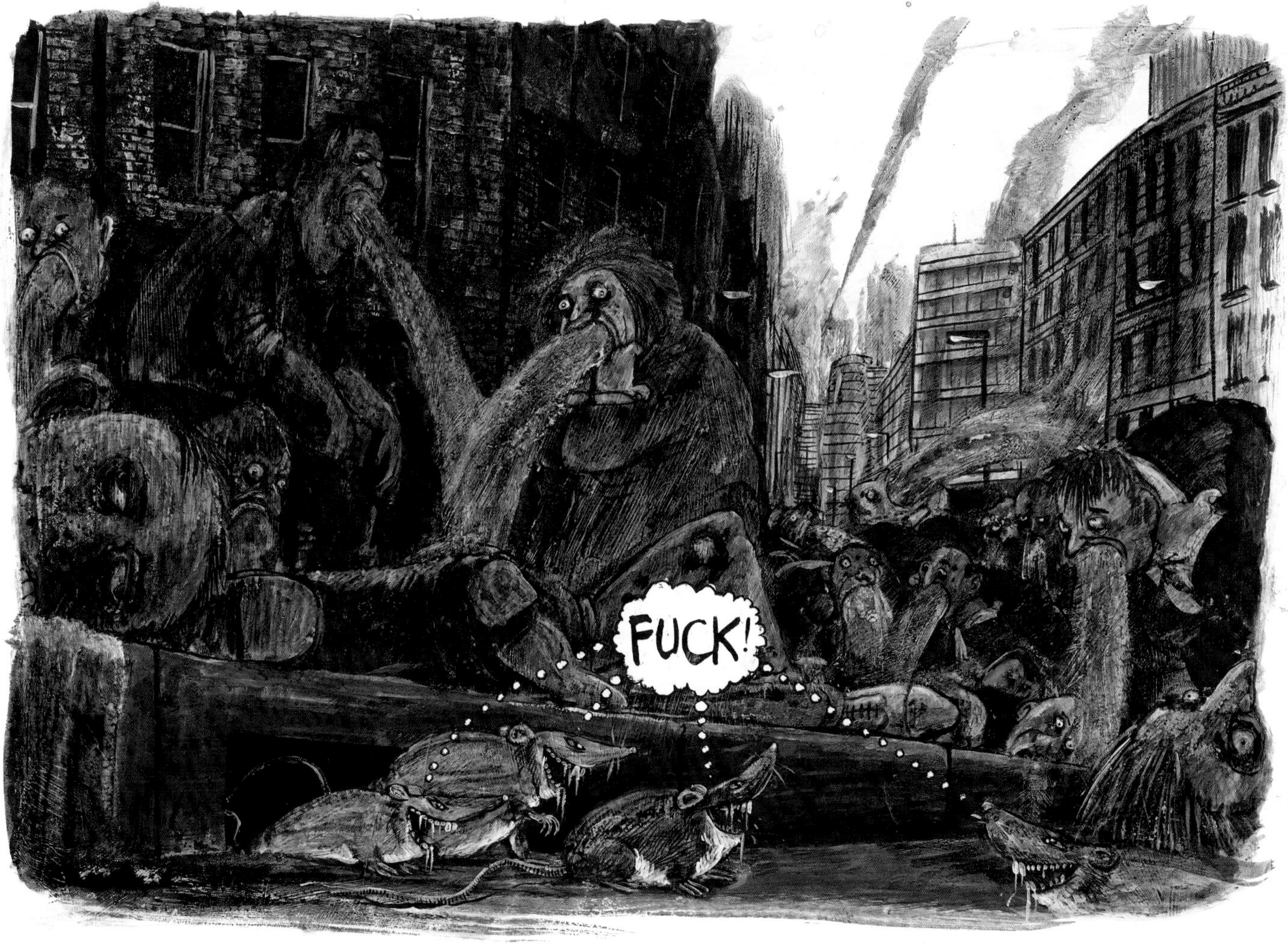
FUCK!

Human Evolution and the Long Awaited Second Coming of Christ

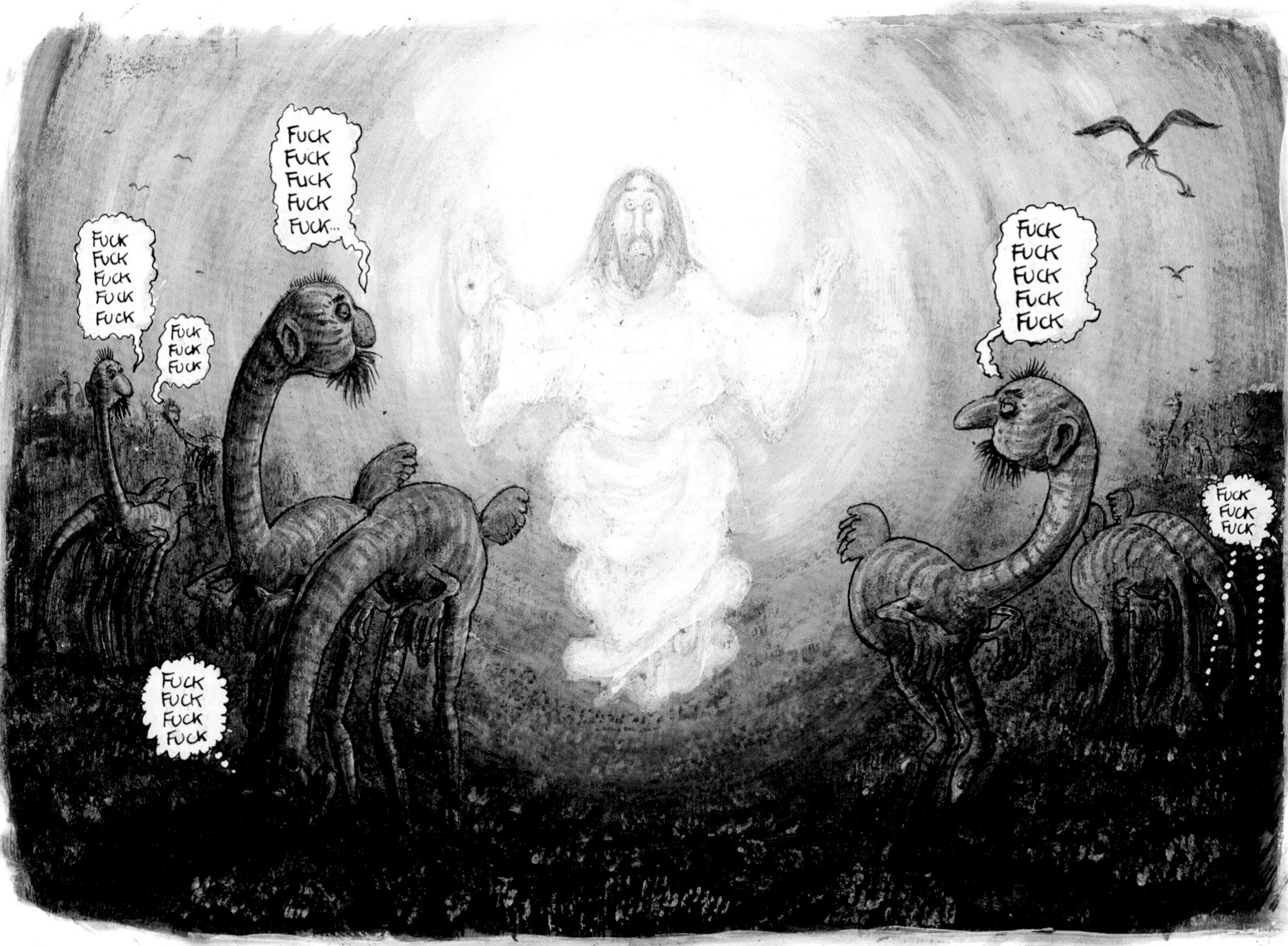
FUCK FUCK FUCK FUCK FUCK
FUCK FUCK FUCK
FUCK FUCK FUCK FUCK FUCK...
FUCK FUCK FUCK FUCK
FUCK FUCK FUCK FUCK FUCK
FUCK FUCK FUCK

The End

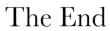

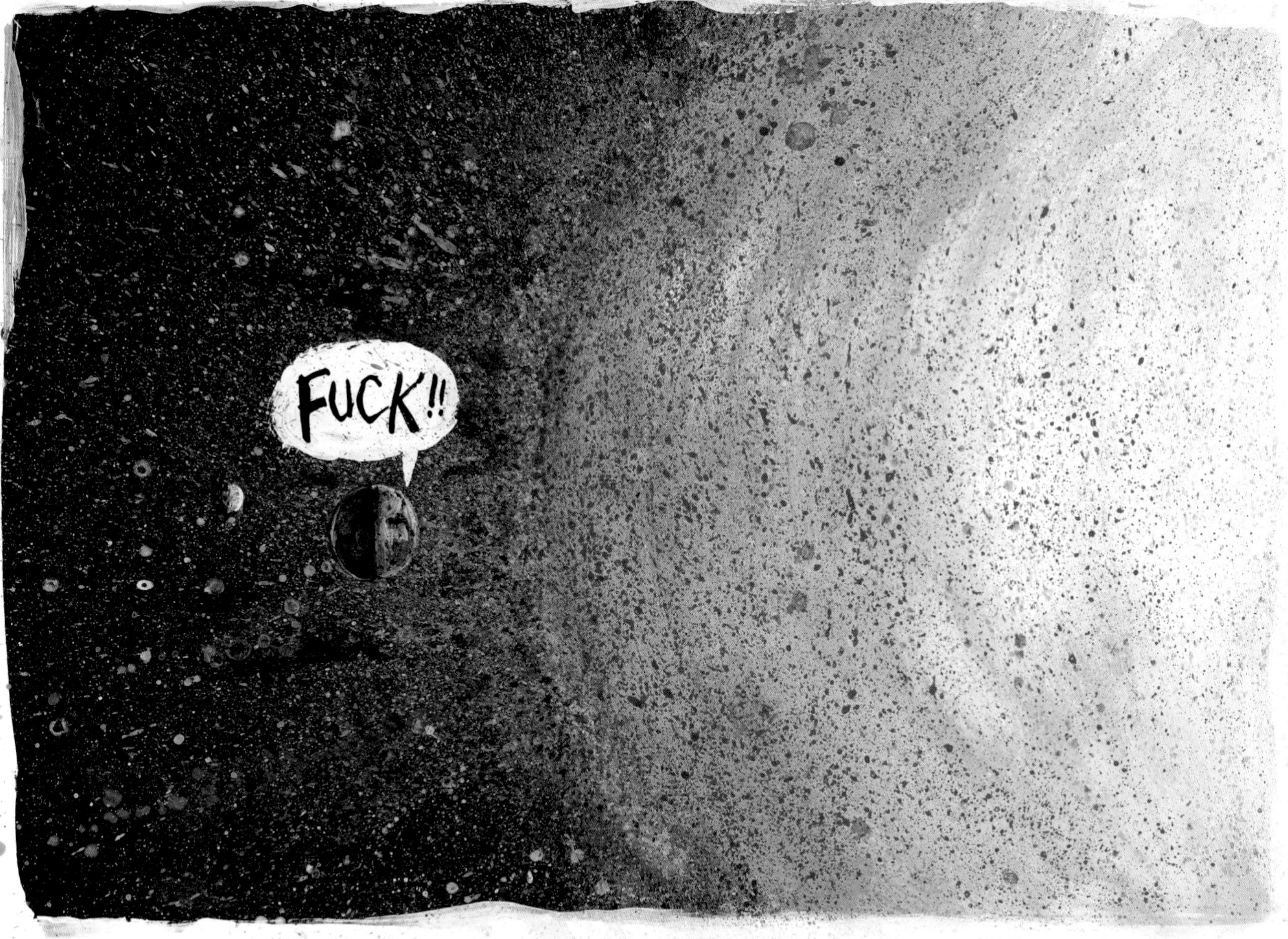
FUCK!!

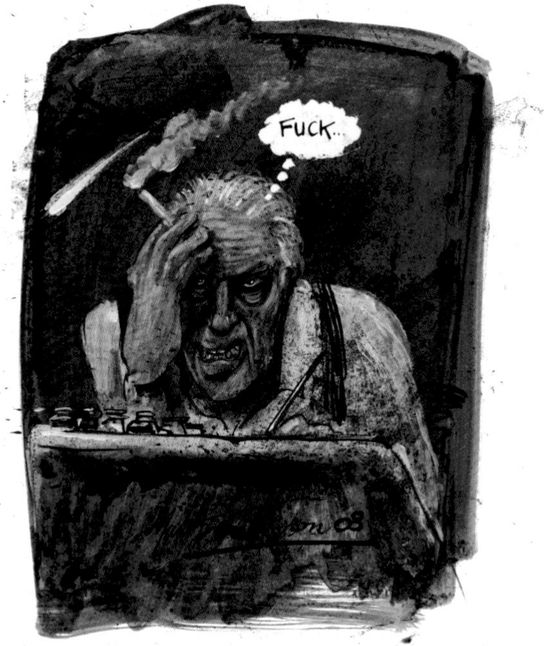
FUCK..

Martin Rowson is an award-winning political cartoonist whose work appears regularly in the *Guardian*, the *Independent on Sunday*, the *Daily Mirror*, the *Scotsman*, *Tribune*, *Index on Censorship*, the *Morning Star* and *The Spectator*. His previous publications include comic-book adaptations of *The Waste Land* and *Tristram Shandy*, a novel, *Snatches*, (2006), and a memoir, *Stuff* (2007). He lives with his wife and their two teenage children in London.